不朽的美

云想衣裳花想容

许渊冲经典英译诗词

（唐朝）

第二辑：汉英对照

Songs of the Immortals

AN ANTHOLOGY OF CLASSICAL CHINESE POETRY (II)

Translated by Xu Yuan Zhong

许渊冲 译

新世界出版社
NEW WORLD PRESS

First Edition 2019

Translated by Xu Yuan Zhong
Designed by He Yuting

ISBN 978-7-5104-6280-1

Published by
NEW WORLD PRESS
24 Baiwanzhuang Street, Beijing 100037, China

Distributed by
NEW WORLD PRESS
24 Baiwanzhuang Street, Beijing 100037, China
Tel: 86-10-68995968
Fax: 86-10-68998705
Website: www.nwp.com.cn
E-mail: nwpcd@sina.com

Printed in the People's Republic of China

目录

INTRODUCTION

"Chinese literature," according to John Turner in his *Golden Treasury of Chinese Poetry*, "is the high artistic peak of the most literary, the most artistic, the longest-established civilization that exists."

I

The Tang Dynasty (618-907) was the golden age of Chinese poetry. It may be divided into four periods: Early Tang (618-712), High Tang (713-770), Middle Tang (771-835) and Late Tang (836-907). Early Tang poetry followed the ornate style of the Six Dynasties, but some poets began to break the tradition. For instance, Yu Shinan (558-638), whom the emperor highly appreciated, wrote the following five-character quatrain called *The Firefly*:

You shed a flickering light;
Your wings are weak in flight.
Afraid to be unknown,

At night you gleam alone.

Later, Wang Bo (c. 649-676) and three other poets tried to develop a style of their own and were criticized by their contemporaries. But Du Fu wrote the following seven-character quatrain in support of them:

Our four great poets have their own creative style;
You shallow critics may make your remarks unfair,
But you will perish with your criticism, while
Their fame will last as the river flows fore'er.

It was Chen Zi'ang (661-702) who succeeded in infusing new vitality into the tradition of the Six Dynasties by returning to the spirit of Han and Wei poetry. He was regarded as a precursor of the High Tang poets.

The High Tang period represented the peak of poetic excellence in the Tang Dynasty. It corresponds roughly to the reign of Emperor Xuan Zong (712-755), a ruler whose early years on the throne were marked by power and splendor and who, as a worshipper of Confucius, wrote the following five-character verse while offering sacrifices to him:

For what did you so busily strive, my Sage,
Expounding hard your doctrine in your age?

Even his favorite Lady Yang could write poems and the following is her seven-character quatrain *Dancing*:

Silk sleeves are swaying ceaselessly with fragrance spread;
In autumn mist are floating lotus lilies red.
Light clouds o'er mountains high ripple with breezes cool;
Young willow shoots caress water of garden pool.

During the reign of Xuan Zong, all civil service examination candidates were required to compose a regulated verse, so poetry became an indispensable accomplishment and a daily accompaniment to the lives of officials and scholars.

Among the High Tang poets, Wang Changling (698-756) was well-known for his seven-character quatrains, in which we can see the influence of the Six Dynasties palace poetry. The following quatrain on a disfavored court lady is typical:

She brings her broom at dawn to dust the golden halls
And strolls about with round fan within the palace walls.
Her rosy color envies wintry crow's black one,
Oft bathed in favorable light of royal sun.

Instead of describing the luxurious palace life in flowery poetic style, this quatrain reveals the poet's sympathy with a disfavored lady whose beauty could not even outshine the ugly crow, so it reads more like *Lament of the Autumn Fan* of the Han Dynasty than a palace poem of the Six Dynasties.

Wang Wei (701-761) was the most important pastoral poet of the

High Tang period, best known for his five-character poems. He was a devout Buddhist, a fact that deeply influenced the way in which he viewed the world and his place in it. As a celebrator of the quiet joys of rural life, he followed a line of development earlier explored by Tao Qian, though he wrote with greater calm and detachment than Tao. For example, his *The Dale of Singing Birds* reads as follows:

I hear osmanthus blooms fall unenjoyed;
When night comes, hills dissolve into the void.
The rising moon arouses birds to sing,
Their fitful twitters fill the dale with spring.

He did not assiduously seek out the picturesque elements in the natural landscape, but rather registered the scenes about him just as they appeared. No wonder it is said "in his poetry there is painting and in his painting there is poetry."

II

Li Bai was the best-known poet in Chinese history, a representative of High Tang culture, the combination of Northern culture represented by Confucian philosophy and *The Book of Poetry* and Southern culture represented by Taoist philosophy and *The Verse of Chu.* His life may be summed up by the following quatrain *To Li Bai* written by Du Fu:

When autumn comes, you're drifting still like thistledown;
You try to find the way to heaven, but you fail.
In singing mad and drinking dead your days you drown.
For whom will fly the roc? For whom will leap the whale?

Li Bai could not fulfil his Confucian ideal to serve the country, spending his later years wandering lonely like a drifting cloud. Nor could he find spiritual freedom in Taoism which taught him to seek the way to heaven. He could but chant poetry and drink wine to drown his sorrows as described by Du Fu in *Eight Immortal Drinkers*:

Li Bai could turn sweet nectar into verses fine.
Drunk in the capital, he'd lie in shops of wine.
Even imperial summons proudly he'd decline,
Saying immortals could not leave the drink divine.

In Li Bai we have the tragedy of a lonely genius wandering the earth like an angel fallen from heaven. When would he realize his aspiration to fly to the sky like the fabulous roc mentioned by the Taoist philosopher Zhuang Zi?

Li Bai's poetry is marked by masculine grandeur (*Watching from Afar the Waterfall on Mount Lu*) and natural grace (*The Moon over Mount Brow*). His imagery may be sublime (the giant bird symbolizing his love of freedom) or graceful (the moon conveying his sympathy to his banished friend Wang Changling). His description of natural scenery is characterized by a swift and fierce imaginative sweep. For instance:

Oh, lightning flashes
And thunder rumbles;
With stunning crashes,
The mountain crumbles.

But he disappoints when describing human feelings and always compares them to natural phenomena. For example:

However deep the Lake of Peach Blossom may be,
It's not so deep, O Wang Lun! as your love for me.

He is little given to expressions of despair or bitterness. His poetry on the whole is calm, at times sunny in outlook. It appears to grow out of certain convictions that he held regarding life and art, out of a tireless search for spiritual freedom and communion with nature as in Poem (*Sitting Alone Facing Peak Jingting*), a lively imagination and a deep sensitivity to beauty (*A Reply to Someone in the Hills*).

> Peach blossoms fallen on the running stream pass by;
> This is an earthly paradise beneath the sky.

III

Du Fu was as great a realistic poet as Li Bai was a romantic. As Li was called "Poet Immortal," Du was remembered by posterity as the "Poet Sage" or "Poet Historian" because he had mirrored in his works the world he lived in and revealed himself with candor and passion. While Li cherished now Confucian then Taoist ideal, Du was imbued with a strong Confucian sense of duty that compelled him to continue serving the Tang Dynasty in the hope of assuaging the ills of the nation. His poetry describes the grief as famine and misrule were inflicting upon his countrymen on the one hand and reproaches those who were responsible for the misery on the other. For instance, he wrote on his way from the capital to Fengxian the following well-known couplet:

> The mansions burst with wine and meat;
> The poor die frozen in the street.

Li Bai also reproached men in power, but he only said:

How can I stoop and bow before the men in power
And so deny myself a happy hour?

These two examples clearly show Li as subjective and romantic and Du as objective and realistic.

The same is true of their descriptions of natural scenery. They both wrote about mountains, but we find in Li's *Mount Skyland* an imaginary mountain "surpassing the Five Peaks" in height, and in Du's *Mount Tai* (one of the Five Peaks) "one boundless green outspread two states." They both described the Yangtze River, Li as "the endless river rolls beyond the azure sky," a view only the mind's eye can yield, while in Du "the endless river rolls its waves from hour to hour," in a description obvious to everyone. They both sailed through the Three Gorges; we find in Li only his own joy, while in Du not only the joy of his family but also that of all the people returning to their homes in the recaptured regions. They both wrote about clouds and birds, but in Li's *Peak Jingting* we seem to see the poet lonely as the cloud and free as the bird, while in Du's *Mount Tai* the poet is only an observer of the rising clouds and the fleeting birds. They both described rain, but Li did not like to see it coming "from dark, dark cloud," while Du felt happy to see it "mutely moisten all."

In expressing feelings, Li was more personal and Du more sympathetic. Both of them felt lonely, but Li was detached in his solitude while Du could not free himself from his attachment to the Tang Dynasty, and this is one of the essential differences between them.

Among other High Tang poets, Cen Shen (715-770) was well-known for his frontier verse ("The frozen red flag in the wind won't undulate"). His ballads with descriptions of the harsh climate and rough terrain of the frontier stand in marked contrast to the pastoral poems of Wang Wei.

IV

If the Early Tang and High Tang periods may be likened to the spring and summer of a year, then the Middle Tang can be compared to autumn, the season of harvest. The revolt of An Lushan in 755 had a disastrous effect on the economic and political life of the Tang Dynasty and it never recovered its former stability. In keeping with the changed nature of the times poetry took on an increasingly autumnal air. On the one hand, Wei Yingwu (737-789) followed the tradition of pastoral poetry (*On the West Stream at Chuzhou*) and on the other, Li Yi (748-827), that of the frontier poems (*On Hearing a Flute at Night atop the Victor's Wall*). But their poetry had not the tone of exuberance that had marked the earlier decades.

The most important poet of the Middle Tang period was Bai Juyi (772-846), who mingled Du Fu's realistic tradition with Li Bai's romanticism (*The Everlasting Regret*), but he also made innovations and wrote "New Music Bureau Ballads" in a style marked by deliberate simplicity (*The White-Haired Palace Maid*). He himself placed high value on his poems of social criticism such as *The Red Cockatoo*:

Annam has sent us from afar a red cockatoo;
Colored like peach-tree blossom, it speaks
as men do,
But it is shut up in a cage with bar on bar
Just as the learned or eloquent scholars are.

This seven-character quatrain, which reveals the relationship between the ruler and the ruled intellectuals, acts more upon the reason than the emotions and may be considered a forerunner of the didactic poetry of the Song Dynasty. Another seven-character quatrain which reveals the Buddhist influence on the poet reads as follows:

Studying the Buddhist doctrine of emptiness, I find
The way to still all common states of mind....

But the great Buddhist influence revolted another Confucian innovator Han Yu (768-824), who submitted to the emperor a memorial in which he reprimanded His Majesty for his devotion to Buddhism and was exiled eight thousand miles away (*Written for My Grandnephew at the Blue Pass*).

Bai Juyi was the most prolific of the Middle Tang poets. As Liu Yuxi (772-842), he composed "Bamboo-Branch Songs" and "Willow-Branch Songs," which are early forms of tuned poetry, that is, a poem or lyric written to a certain tune whose title refers simply to the metrical pattern and in most cases has nothing to do with the poem's content. The tuned lyric marked by lines of varying length came to prominence in the Middle Tang period. For example, Zhang Zhihe's (730-810) *Fisherman's Song* was so widespread that even the Japanese emperor (r. 804-832) wrote five lyrics to the same tune. Zhang's lyric is pastoral, Liu's *Ripples Sifting Sand* realistic and Bai's *Flower in the Haze* symbolic.

V

Li He (790-816) who followed the romantic tradition of Qu Yuan and Li Bai, and whose rich, allusion-laden poetry is obscure and even depressing, may be regarded as a precursor of Late Tang poets. If the major poets of the High Tang were Li Bai and Du Fu, then those of the Late Tang were another Li and Du, that is, Du Mu (803-852) and Li Shangyin (812-858).

Du Mu has shunned in his poetry "the ornate and the strange" on the one hand and "the commonplace and the vulgar" on the other. His seven-character quatrains are admired for their visual immediacy and delicacy of feelings. For instance, one of his farewell poems reads:

Deep, deep our love, too deep to show.
Deep, deep we drink; silent we grow.
The candle grieves to see us part;
It melts in tears with burnt-out heart.

Li Shangyin was perhaps the most influential of all the Late Tang poets. His seven-character regulated verse reads like Du Fu's and Han Yu's in syntax and structure, and like Li He's in diction and allusiveness. He is well-known for his ambiguous or obscure poems, often untitled, dealing with clandestine love. He was the first poet to write love poems in the modern sense and has left to posterity such unforgettable couplets as:

The silkworm till its death spins silk from lovesick heart;
The candle when, consumed has no more tears to shed.
The setting sun appears sublime,
But O! 'Tis near its dying time.

The second couplet may be said to be the epitome of Late Tang poetry.

Wen Tingyun (813-870) was the most important lyricist or composer of tuned lyrics of the Late Tang; he transformed them from mere songs of entertainment to verses of high literary quality. In his lyrics two main styles are predominate: a richly embellished depiction of the abandoned woman as opposed to the court lady in the palace poem, and a simple narration in the folk song manner as represented by *Dreaming of the South.*

Wei Zhuang (836-910) was another important lyricist of the period of transition. His tuned lyrics are straightforward, narrative and colloquial, directly expressing personal feelings and autobiographical details as opposed to Wen's indirect depiction of feminine feelings.

What he adds to the tuned lyric reveals a reaction against the ornate style of Wen, who excels in writing poems with implicit meaning, while Wei is famed for explicit poetry.

In 881, Huang Chao (?-884) led an army of sixty thousand peasant rebels into the Tang capital and proclaimed himself emperor. He expressed his ambition in *The Chrysanthemum*, with whose "golden armor plates" came the end of the Tang Dynasty.

TANG DYNASTY

(618-907)

唐朝

（618—907）

YU SHINAN
(558-638)

The Firefly

You shed a flickering light;
Your wings are weak in flight.
Afraid to be unknown,
At night you gleam alone.

虞世南
（*558–638*）

咏萤

的历流光小，
飘摇弱翅轻。
恐畏无人识，
独自暗中明。

KONG SHAO'AN
(577-622)

Falling Leaves

In early autumn I'm sad to see falling leaves;
They're dreary like a roamer's heart that their fall grieves.
They twist and twirl as if struggling against the breeze;
I seem to hear them cry, "We will not leave our trees."

孔绍安
（577–622）

落叶

早秋惊落叶，
飘零似客心。
翻飞未肯下，
犹言惜故林。

WANG JI
(c. 589-644)

The Wineshop*

Drinking wine all day long,
I won't keep my mind sane.
Seeing the drunken throng,
Should I sober remain?

* Written during the war that preceded the Tang Dynasty.

王绩

（约 589–644）

过酒家

此日长昏饮，

非关养性灵。

眼看人尽醉，

何忍独为醒？

MONK OF COLD HILL
(Dates Unknown)

Long, Long the Pathway to Cold Hill

Long, long the pathway to Cold Hill;
Drear, drear the waterside so chill.
Chirp, chirp, I often hear the bird;
Mute, mute, nobody says a word.
Gust by gust winds caress my face;
Flake on flake snow covers all trace.
From day to day the sun won't shine;
From year to year no spring is mine.

寒山

（生卒年不详）

杳杳寒山道

杳杳寒山道，落落冷涧滨。

啾啾常有鸟，寂寂更无人。

淅淅风吹面，纷纷雪积身。

朝朝不见日，岁岁不知春。

WANG BO
(c. 649-676)

Prince Teng's Pavilion

By riverside* towers Prince Teng's Pavilion proud,
But gone are cabs with ringing bells and stirring strains.
At dawn its painted beams bar the south-flying cloud;
At dusk its curtains furled face western mountains' rains.
Free clouds cast shadows in the pool from day to day;
The world and seasons change beneath the changing sky.
Where is the prince who in this pavilion did stay?
Beyond the balustrade the silent river rolls by.

* By the side of the Gan River in present-day Nanchang, Jiangxi Province.

王勃
（约 649–676）

滕王阁诗

滕王高阁临江渚，佩玉鸣鸾罢歌舞。
画栋朝飞南浦云，珠帘暮卷西山雨。
闲云潭影日悠悠，物换星移几度秋。
阁中帝子今何在？槛外长江空自流。

Farewell to Prefect Du

You'll leave the town walled far and wide
For mist-veiled land by riverside.
I feel on parting sad and drear,
For both of us are strangers here.
If you've a friend who knows your heart,
Distance can't keep you two apart.
At crossroads where we bid adieu,
Do not shed tears as women do!

送杜少府之任蜀州

城阙辅三秦，风烟望五津。
与君离别意，同是宦游人。
海内存知己，天涯若比邻。
无为在歧路，儿女共沾巾。

YANG JIONG
(650-695?)

I Would Rather Fight

The beacon fire shines o'er the capital,
My agitated mind can't be calmed down.
By royal order we leave palace hall;
Our armored steeds besiege the Dragon Town.
Snow darkens pictures sewn on banners red;
In howling winds are mingled our drumbeats.
I'd rather fight at a hundred men's head
Than pore o'er books without performing feats.

杨炯

（650–695?）

从军行

烽火照西京，心中自不平。
牙璋辞凤阙，铁骑绕龙城。
雪暗凋旗画，风多杂鼓声。
宁为百夫长，胜作一书生。

LUO BINWANG
(c. 638-?)

The Cicada Heard in Prison

In autumn the cicada sings;
A prisoner, I'm lost in thought.
I cannot bear to see its dark wings,
Which to my head white hair have brought.
Heavy with dew, it cannot fly;
Drowned in the wind, its song's not heard.
No one believes its spirit high.
Who could express my grief in word?

骆宾王

（约 638– ？）

在狱咏蝉

西陆蝉声唱，南冠客思深。
不堪玄鬓影，来对白头吟。
露重飞难进，风多响易沉。
无人信高洁，谁为表予心？

WEI CHENGQING
(?-707)

Southbound, I Part from My Younger Brother

On and on flows the River Long;
Deep and deep grows our grief to part.
The flowers fall mute all along
As if they too were sad at heart.

韦承庆
（?–707）

南行别弟

澹澹长江水，
悠悠远客情。
落花相与恨，
到地一无声。

SONG ZHIWEN
(656-712)

Crossing the River Han*

Exiled, I longed for news none bring,
From the long winter to late spring.
Now nearing home, timid I grow,
I dare not ask what I would know.

* In present-day Hubei Province.

宋之问

（656–712）

渡汉江

岭外音书断，

经冬复历春。

近乡情更怯，

不敢问来人。

SHEN QUANQI
(656-714)

The Garrison at Yellow Dragon Town

Stationed at Yellow Dragon Town, the men
Have never been relieved year after year.
At home their wives are watching the moon, when
They're staying in the camp on the frontier.
Their wives are longing for them when spring comes
And can't forget their love on parting night.
Oh, who will lead our troops with flags and drums
To put the foe at Dragon Town to flight!

沈佺期
(656–714)

杂诗

闻道黄龙戍，频年不解兵。
可怜闺里月，长在汉家营。
少妇今春意，良人昨夜情。
谁能将旗鼓，一为取龙城？

HE ZHIZHANG
(659-744)

The Willow

The slender tree is dressed in emerald all about,
A thousand branches droop like fringes made of jade.
But do you know by whom these slim leaves are cut out?
The wind of early spring is sharp as scissor blade.

Homecoming

Old, I return to the homeland I left while young,
Thinner has grown my hair, though I speak the same tongue.
My children, whom I meet, do not know who am I.
"Where are you from, dear sir?" they ask with beaming eye.

贺知章
（659–744）

咏柳

碧玉妆成一树高，万条垂下绿丝绦。
不知细叶谁裁出，二月春风似剪刀。

回乡偶书

少小离家老大回，乡音无改鬓毛衰。
儿童相见不相识，笑问客从何处来？

CHEN ZI'ANG
(661-702)

On Climbing the Tower at Youzhou

Where are the great men of the past?
Where are those of future years?
The sky and earth forever last;
Here and now I alone shed tears.

陈子昂
（661–702）

登幽州台歌

前不见古人，
后不见来者。
念天地之悠悠，
独怆然而涕下！

ZHANG YUE
(667-730)

My Delayed Departure for Home

My heart outruns the moon and sun;
It makes the journey not begun.
The autumn wind won't wait for me;
It arrives there where I would be.

张说
（667–730）

蜀道后期

客心争日月，

来往预期程。

秋风不相待，

先至洛阳城。

ZHANG JIULING
(673-740)

Since My Lord from Me Parted

Since my lord from me parted,
I've left unused my loom.
The moon wanes, brokenhearted,
To see my growing gloom.

张九龄

（673–740）

自君之出矣

自君之出矣，
不复理残机。
思君如满月，
夜夜减清辉。

ZHANG RUOXU
(c. 647-730)

A Moonlit Night on the Spring River

In spring the river rises as high as the sea,
And with the river's rise the moon uprises bright.
She follows the rolling waves for ten thousand li,
And where the river flows, there overflows her light.

The river winds around the fragrant islet where
The blooming flowers in her light all look like snow.
You cannot tell her beams from hoar frost in the air,
Nor from white sand upon Farewell Beach below.

No dust has stained the water blending with the skies;
A lonely wheel-like moon shines brilliant far and wide.
Who by the riverside first saw the moon arise?
When did the moon first see a man by riverside?

Ah, generations have come and passed away;
From year to year the moons look alike, old and new.
We do not know tonight for whom she sheds her ray,
But hear the river say to its water adieu.

张若虚
（约 647–730）

春江花月夜

春江潮水连海平，海上明月共潮生。
滟滟随波千万里，何处春江无月明？
江流宛转绕芳甸，月照花林皆似霰。
空里流霜不觉飞，汀上白沙看不见。

江天一色无纤尘，皎皎空中孤月轮。
江畔何人初见月？江月何年初照人？
人生代代无穷已，江月年年只相似。
不知江月待何人，但见长江送流水。

Away, away is sailing a single cloud white;
On Farewell Beach pine away maples green.
Where is the wanderer sailing his boat tonight?
Who, pining away, on the moonlit rails would lean?

Alas! The moon is lingering over the tower;
It should have seen the dressing table of the fair.
She rolls the curtain up and light comes in her bower;
She washes but can't wash away the moonbeams there.

She sees the moon, but her beloved is out of sight;
She'd follow it to shine on her beloved one's face.
But message-bearing swans can't fly out of moonlight,
Nor can letter-sending fish leap out of their place.

Last night he dreamed that falling flowers would not stay.
Alas! He can't go home, although half spring has gone.
The running water bearing spring will pass away;
The moon declining over the pool will sink anon.

The moon declining sinks into a heavy mist;
It's a long way between southern rivers and eastern seas.
How many can go home by moonlight who are missed?
The sinking moon sheds yearning o'er riverside trees.

白云一片去悠悠，青枫浦上不胜愁。
谁家今夜扁舟子？何处相思明月楼？
可怜楼上月徘徊，应照离人妆镜台。
玉户帘中卷不去，捣衣砧上拂还来。

此时相望不相闻，愿逐月华流照君。
鸿雁长飞光不度，鱼龙潜跃水成文。
昨夜闲潭梦落花，可怜春半不还家。

江水流春去欲尽，江潭落月复西斜。
斜月沉沉藏海雾，碣石潇湘无限路。
不知乘月几人归，落月摇情满江树。

WANG WAN
(c. 693-751)

Passing by the Northern Mountains

My boat goes by the green, green mountainside;
It glides over blue, blue water with ease.
The banks are pushed far back at full tide;*
A single sail seems hanging in the breeze.
The sun emerges ere night has passed away,
And spring intrudes to ring out the old year.
Who'll send my letter home without delay?
I see no northward-flying wild geese here. **

* Weng Xianliang's translation.
** Wild geese were believed to be message-bearing birds.

王湾
（约 693–751）

次北固山下

客路青山外，行舟绿水前。
潮平两岸阔，风正一帆悬。
海日生残夜，江春入旧年。
乡书何处达？归雁洛阳边。

WANG HAN
(687-726)

Starting for the Front

From cups of jade that glow with wine of grapes at night,
Drinking to pipa songs, we are summoned to fight.
Don't laugh if we lie drunk upon the battleground!
How many warriors ever came back safe and sound?

王翰

（687–726）

凉州词

葡萄美酒夜光杯，
欲饮琵琶马上催。
醉卧沙场君莫笑，
古来征战几人回？

WANG ZHIHUAN
(688-742)

On the Heron Tower

The sun beyond the mountains glows;
The Yellow River seawards flows.
You can enjoy a grander sight
By climbing to a greater height.

Out of the Great Wall

The yellow sand rises as high as white cloud;
The lonely town is lost amid the mountains proud.
Why should the Mongol flute complain no willows grow?
Beyond the Jade Gate vernal wind will never blow!

王之涣

（688–742）

登鹳雀楼

白日依山尽，黄河入海流。
欲穷千里目，更上一层楼。

凉州词

黄河远上白云间，一片孤城万仞山。
羌笛何须怨杨柳？春风不度玉门关。

MENG HAORAN
(689-740)

Spring Morning

This morn of spring in bed I'm lying,
Not to awake till birds are crying.
After one night of wind and showers,
How many are the fallen flowers!

Mooring on the River at Jiande

My boat is moored by mist-veiled river shore;
I'm grieved to see the setting sun no more:
On boundless plain clouds hang atop the tree;
In water clear the moon seems near to me.

孟浩然
（689–740）

春晓

春眠不觉晓，处处闻啼鸟。
夜来风雨声，花落知多少。

宿建德江

移舟泊烟渚，日暮客愁新。
野旷天低树，江清月近人。

LI QI
(690-751)

An Old War Song

We climb the hill by day to watch for beacon fires
And water horses by riverside when day expires.
We strike the gong in sand-darkened land where wind blows
And hear the pipa tell the Princess'* secret woes.
There is no town for miles and miles but tents in a row;
Beyond the desert there's nothing but rain and snow.
The wild geese honk from night to night, that's all we hear;
We see but Tatar soldiers shedding tear on tear.
'Tis said we cannot go back through the Jade-Gate Pass,
We'd risk our lives to follow war chariots, alas!
The dead are buried in the desert year on year,
Only to bring back grapes from over the frontier.

* The Princess refers to the beautiful Lady Wang Zhaojun, who was married upon royal order to the Khan of the Tatar tribe in 33 BC

李颀

（690–751）

古从军行

白日登山望烽火，黄昏饮马傍交河。
行人刁斗风沙暗，公主琵琶幽怨多。
野云万里无城郭，雨雪纷纷连大漠。
胡雁哀鸣夜夜飞，胡儿眼泪双双落。
闻道玉门犹被遮，应将性命逐轻车。
年年战骨埋荒外，空见蒲桃入汉家。

WANG CHANGLING
(698-756)

On the Frontier

The moon o'er mountain pass is still the moon of yore;
The men who went to guard the pass are now no more.
Were Flying General* still in Dragon City here,
No Tatar steed would dare to cross the north frontier.

Sorrow of a Young Bride in Her Boudoir

Nothing in her boudoir brings sorrow to the bride;
She mounts the tower, gaily dressed, on a spring day.
Suddenly seeing willows green by the roadside,
Oh, she regrets her lord seeking fame far away!

* Flying General Li Guang (died in AD 125) of the Han Dynasty was much dreaded by the Tatar tribesmen.

王昌龄
（698–756）

出塞

秦时明月汉时关，万里长征人未还。
但使龙城飞将在，不教胡马度阴山。

闺怨

闺中少妇不知愁，春日凝妆上翠楼。
忽见陌头杨柳色，悔教夫婿觅封侯。

WANG WEI
(701-761)

The Deer Enclosure

In pathless hills no man's in sight,
But I still hear echoing sound.
In gloomy forest peeps no light,
But sunbeams slant on mossy ground.

The Dale of Singing Birds

I hear osmanthus blooms fall unenjoyed,
When night comes, hills dissolve into the void.
The rising moon arouses birds to sing,
Their fitful twitters fill the dale with spring.

王维

（701–761）

鹿柴

空山不见人，但闻人语响。

返景入深林，复照青苔上。

鸟鸣涧

人闲桂花落，夜静春山空。

月出惊山鸟，时鸣春涧中。

Parting among the Hills

I watch you leave the hills, compeer;
At dusk I close my wicket door.
When grass turns green in spring next year,
Will you return with spring once more?

Love Seeds

Red berries grow in southern land.
How many load in spring the trees!
Gather them till full is your hand;
They would revive fond memories.

山中送别

山中相送罢，日暮掩柴扉。
春草明年绿，王孙归不归？

相思

红豆生南国，春来发几枝？
愿君多采撷，此物最相思。

Blue Fields in Mist or Rain

O'er pebbles grey a blue stream glides;
Red leaves are strewn on jade hillsides.
Along the path it rains unseen;
My gown grows moist with drizzling green.

Thinking of My Brothers on Mountain-Climbing Day

Alone, a lonely stranger in a foreign land,
I pine for kinsfolk doubly on a holiday.
I know my brothers would, with dogwood spray* in hand,
Climb the mountain and think of me so far away.

A Farewell Song

The little town is quiet after morning rain;
No dust has dulled the tavern willows fresh and green.
I would ask you to drink a cup of wine again;
West of the Sunny Pass no more friends will be seen.

* A dogwood spray carried on mountain-climbing day, that is, the ninth day of the ninth lunar month, was supposed to drive away evil spirits.

山中

荆溪白石出，天寒红叶稀。
山路元无雨，空翠湿人衣。

九月九日忆山东兄弟

独在异乡为异客，每逢佳节倍思亲。
遥知兄弟登高处，遍插茱萸少一人。

送元二使安西

渭城朝雨浥轻尘，客舍青青柳色新。
劝君更尽一杯酒，西出阳关无故人。

WANG YA
(764-835)

Farewell to Spring

From day to day man will grow old,
So drink the cup of wine you hold!
Don't grieve o'er flowers falling here;
They'll come with spring from year to year.

王涯

（764–835）

送春辞

日日人空老，
年年春更归。
相欢在尊酒，
不用惜花飞。

LIU SHENXU
(c. 714-767)

A Scholar's Retreat

The pathway ends where white clouds rise;
Spring reigns as far as Blue Stream goes.
Now and then fragrant flower flies;
Where water runs, its fragrance flows.
The pathway leads to doors oft shut;
A study's shaded by willow trees.
From dazzling sun is screened the hut;
Soft light is filtered by the breeze.

刘眘虚

（约 714–767）

阙题

道由白云尽，春与青溪长。

时有落花至，远随流水香。

闲门向山路，深柳读书堂。

幽映每白日，清辉照衣裳。

LI BAI
(701-762)

The Moon over Mount Brow

The crescent moon shines bright like autumn's golden brow;
Its deep reflection flows with limpid water blue.
I'll leave the town on Clear Stream for Three Gorges now.
O Moon, how I miss you when you are out of view!*

Watching from Afar the Waterfall on Mount Lu

The sunlit Censer Peak exhales a wreath of cloud;
Like an upended stream the cataract sounds loud.
Its torrent dashes down three thousand feet from high,
As if the Silver River** fell from azure sky.

* The moon was screened from view by riverside cliffs.
** The Chinese name for the Milky Way.

李白

（701–762）

峨眉山月歌

峨眉山月半轮秋，影入平羌江水流。

夜发清溪向三峡，思君不见下渝州。

望庐山瀑布

日照香炉生紫烟，遥看瀑布挂前川。

飞流直下三千尺，疑是银河落九天。

A Trader's Wife

My forehead covered by my hair cut straight,
I played with flowers pluck'd before the gate.
On hobbyhorse you came upon the scene,
Around the well we played with mumes still green.
We lived, close neighbors on Riverside Lane,
Carefree and innocent, we children twain.
At fourteen years when I became your bride,
I'd often turn my bashful face aside.
Hanging my head, I'd look towards the wall,
A thousand times I'd not answer your call.
At fifteen years when I composed my brows,
To mix my dust with yours were my dear vows.
Rather than break faith, you declared you'd die.
Who knew I'd live alone in a tower high?
I was sixteen when you went far away,
Passing Three Gorges studded with rocks grey,
Where ships were wrecked when spring flood ran high,
Where gibbons' wails seemed coming from the sky.
Green moss now overgrows before our door,
Your footprints, hidden, can be seen no more.
Moss can't be swept away, so thick it grows,
And leaves fall early when the west wind blows.
The yellow butterflies in autumn pass
Two by two o'er our western garden grass.
This sight would break my heart and I'm afraid,
Sitting alone, my rosy cheeks would fade.
Oh, when are you to leave the Western land?
Do not forget to let me know beforehand!
I'll walk to meet you and not call it far
To go to Long Wind Sands or where you are.

长干行

妾发初覆额，折花门前剧。
郎骑竹马来，绕床弄青梅。
同居长干里，两小无嫌猜。
十四为君妇，羞颜未尝开。
低头向暗壁，千唤不一回。
十五始展眉，愿同尘与灰。
常存抱柱信，岂上望夫台。
十六君远行，瞿塘滟滪堆。
五月不可触，猿声天上哀。
门前迟行迹，一一生绿苔。
苔深不能扫，落叶秋风早。
八月蝴蝶黄，双飞西园草。
感此伤妾心，坐愁红颜老。
早晚下三巴，预将书报家。
相迎不道远，直至长风沙。

Thoughts on a Silent Night

Before my bed a pool of light–
Can it be frost upon the ground?
Eyes raised, I see the moon so bright;
Head bent, in homesickness I'm drowned.

Seeing Meng Haoran Off at Yellow Crane Tower

My friend has left the west where towers Yellow Crane
For River Town while willows down and flowers reign.
His lessening sail is lost in the boundless azure sky,
Where I see but the endless river rolling by.

静夜思

床前明月光，疑是地上霜。

举头望明月，低头思故乡。

黄鹤楼送孟浩然之广陵

故人西辞黄鹤楼，烟花三月下扬州。

孤帆远影碧空尽，唯见长江天际流。

Invitation to Wine

Do you not see the Yellow River come from the sky,
Rushing into the sea and ne'er come back?
Do you not see the mirror bright in chamber high
Grieve o'er your snow-white hair that once was silken black?
When hopes are won, oh, drink your fill in high delight
And never leave your wine cup empty in moonlight!
Heaven has made us talents; we're not made in vain.
A thousand gold coins spent, more will turn up again.
Kill a cow, cook a sheep and let us merry be,
And drink three hundred cupfuls of wine in high glee!
Dear friends of mine,
Cheer up, cheer up!
I invite you to wine.
Do not put down your cup!
I will sing you a song, please hear,
O hear! Lend me a willing ear!
What difference will rare and costly dishes make?
I want only to get drunk and never to wake.
How many great men were forgotten through the ages?
Great drinkers are better known than sober sages.
The Prince of Poets* feasted in his palace at will,
Drank wine at ten thousand coins a cask and laughed his fill.
A host should not complain of money he is short;
To drink together we'd sell things of any sort.
The fur coat worth a thousand coins of gold
And flower-dappled horse may both be sold
To buy good wine that we may drown the woes age-old.

---

* Cao Zhi, prince of the Kingdom of Wei (see note to Cao Zhi's poems).

将进酒

君不见黄河之水天上来，奔流到海不复回！
君不见高堂明镜悲白发，朝如青丝暮成雪！
人生得意须尽欢，莫使金樽空对月。
天生我材必有用，千金散尽还复来。
烹羊宰牛且为乐，会须一饮三百杯。
岑夫子，丹丘生，将进酒，杯莫停。
与君歌一曲，请君为我倾耳听。
钟鼓馔玉不足贵，但愿长醉不复醒。
古来圣贤皆寂寞，惟有饮者留其名。
陈王昔时宴平乐，斗酒十千恣欢谑。
主人何为言少钱，径须沽取对君酌。
五花马，千金裘，
呼儿将出换美酒，与尔同销万古愁。

Drinking Alone Under the Moon

Among the flowers from a pot of wine
I drink alone beneath the bright moonshine.
I raise my cup to invite the moon, who blends
Her light with my shadow and we're three friends.
The moon does not know how to drink her share;
In vain my shadow follows me here and there.
Together with them for the time I stay
And make merry before spring's spent away.
I sing the moon to linger with my song;
My shadow disperses as I dance along.
Sober, we three remain cheerful and gay;
Drunken, we part and each goes his way.
Our friendship will outshine all earthly love;
Next time we'll meet beyond the stars above.

月下独酌

花间一壶酒，独酌无相亲。
举杯邀明月，对影成三人。
月既不解饮，影徒随我身。
暂伴月将影，行乐须及春。
我歌月徘徊，我舞影零乱。
醒时同交欢，醉后各分散。
永结无情游，相期邈云汉。

Mount Skyland Ascended in a Dream–A Song of Farewell

Of fairy isles seafarers speak,
'Mid dimming mist and surging waves, so hard to seek;
Of Skyland southerners are proud,
Perceivable through fleeting or dispersing cloud.
Mount Skyland threatens heaven, massed against the sky,
Surpassing the Five Peaks and dwarfing Mount Red Town.
Mount Heaven's Terrace, five hundred thousand feet high,
Nearby to the southeast, appears to crumble down.
Longing in dreams for southern land, one night
I flew o'er Mirror Lake in moonlight.
My shadow's followed by moonbeams
Until I reach Shimmering Streams,
Where hermitage of Master Xie* can still be seen
And gibbons wail o'er rippling water green.
I put on Xie's pegged boot,
One on each foot,
And scale the mountain ladder to blue cloud.
On eastern cliff I see
The sun rise from the sea
And in midair I hear sky cock crow loud.
The footpath meanders 'mid a thousand crags in the vale;
I'm lured by rocks and flowers when the day turns pale.
Bears roar and dragons howl and thunders the cascade;
Deep forests quake and ridges tremble; they're afraid.

* Xie Lingyun (385-433), a Jin Dynasty poet who was fond of mountaineering and made himself special pegged boots for climbing.

梦游天姥吟留别

海客谈瀛洲，烟涛微茫信难求。
越人语天姥，云霞明灭或可睹。
天姥连天向天横，势拔五岳掩赤城。
天台四万八千丈，对此欲倒东南倾。
我欲因之梦吴越，一夜飞度镜湖月。
湖月照我影，送我至剡溪。
谢公宿处今尚在，渌水荡漾清猿啼。
脚著谢公屐，身登青云梯。
半壁见海日，空中闻天鸡。
千岩万转路不定，迷花倚石忽已暝。
熊咆龙吟殷岩泉，栗深林兮惊层巅。

From dark, dark cloud comes rain;
On pale, pale waves mists plane.
Oh, lightning flashes
And thunder rumbles;
With stunning crashes
The mountain crumbles.
The stone gate of a fairy cavern under
Suddenly breaks asunder.
So blue, so deep, so vast appears an endless sky,
Where sun and moon shine on gold and silver terraces high.
Clad in the rainbow, riding on the wind,
The Lords of Clouds descend in a procession long.
Their chariots drawn by phoenix disciplined,
And tigers playing for them a zither song,
Row upon row, like fields of hemp, immortals throng.
Suddenly my heart and soul stirred, I
Awake with long, long sighs.
I find my head on pillow lies
And fair visions have gone by.
Likewise all human joys will pass away
Just as east-flowing water of olden day.
I'll take my leave of you, not knowing for how long;
I'll tend a white deer among
The grassy slopes of the green hill
So that I may ride it to famous mountains at will.
How can I stoop and bow before the men in power
And so deny myself a happy hour?

云青青兮欲雨，水澹澹兮生烟。

列缺霹雳，丘峦崩摧。

洞天石扉，訇然中开。

青冥浩荡不见底，日月照耀金银台。

霓为衣兮风为马，云之君兮纷纷而来下。

虎鼓瑟兮鸾回车，仙之人兮列如麻。

忽魂悸以魄动，恍惊起而长嗟。

惟觉时之枕席，失向来之烟霞。

世间行乐亦如此，古来万事东流水。

别君去兮何时还？

且放白鹿青崖间，须行即骑访名山。

安能摧眉折腰事权贵，使我不得开心颜！

Sitting Alone Facing Peak Jingting

All birds have flown away, so high;
A lonely cloud drifts on, so free.
Gazing at Peak Jingting, nor I
Am tired of him, nor he of me.

Farewell to a Friend

Green mountains bar the northern sky;
White water girds the eastern town.
Here is the place to say good-bye;
You'll drift like lonely thistle down.
With floating cloud you'll float away;
Like parting day I'll part from you.
We wave as you start on your way;
Our steeds still neigh, "Adieu, adieu!"

独坐敬亭山

众鸟高飞尽，孤云独去闲。
相看两不厌，只有敬亭山。

送友人

青山横北郭，白水绕东城。
此地一为别，孤蓬万里征。
浮云游子意，落日故人情。
挥手自兹去，萧萧班马鸣。

CUI HAO
(c. 704-754)

Yellow Crane Tower

The sage on yellow crane was gone amid clouds white.
To what avail is Yellow Crane Tower left here?
Once gone, the yellow crane will ne'er on earth alight;
Only white clouds still float in vain from year to year.
By sunlit river trees can be counted one by one;
On Parrot Islet sweet green grass grows fast and thick.
Where is my native land beyond the setting sun?
The mist-veiled waves of River Han make me homesick.

崔颢

（约 704–754）

黄鹤楼

昔人已乘黄鹤去，此地空余黄鹤楼。

黄鹤一去不复返，白云千载空悠悠。

晴川历历汉阳树，芳草萋萋鹦鹉洲。

日暮乡关何处是？烟波江上使人愁。

ZHANG XU*
(c. 675-750)

To a Guest in the Hills

On all things in the hills spring sheds a golden light.
Do not go back when shady rain clouds come in sight.
Even on a fine day when the sun shines bright,
Your gown will moisten in the thick of clouds white.

* A famous calligrapher of whom a description may be found in Du Fu's poem "Eight Immortal Drinkers."

张旭
（约 675–750）

山中留客

山光物态弄春晖，
莫为轻阴便拟归。
纵使晴明无雨色，
入云深处亦沾衣。

CHANG JIAN
(708-?)

A Buddhist Retreat in a Ruined Mountain Temple

I come to an ancient temple at first light;
The lofty trees are steeped in sunbeams white.
A winding footpath leads to deep retreat,
Where Dhyana Cell is hid 'mid flowers sweet.
In mountain's aura flying birds feel pleasure;
In shaded pool the carefree mind finds leisure.
All worldly sounds are hushed here and there,
But chimes of bells still linger in the air.

常建

（708–？）

破山寺后禅院

清晨入古寺，初日照高林。

曲径通幽处，禅房花木深。

山光悦鸟性，潭影空人心。

万籁此俱寂，但余钟磬音。

GAO SHI
(706-765)

Song of the Northern Frontier

A cloud of smoke and dust spreads o'er northeast frontier;
To fight the remnant foe our generals leave the rear.
Brave men should go no matter where beneath the sky;
The emperor bestows on them his favor high.
To the beat of drum and gong through Elm Pass they go,
Round Mount Stone Tablet flags serpentine row on row.
But urgent orders speed over the Sea of Sand;
Mount Wolf aflame with fires set by the Tatar band.
Both hills and streams are desolate on border plain;
The Tatar horsemen flurry like the wind and rain.
Half our warriors lie killed on the battleground,
While pretty girls in camp still sing and dance their round.
Grass withers in the desert as autumn is late;
At sunset few men guard the lonely city gate.
Imperial favor makes them hold the foemen light;
Their town is under siege, though they've fought with all their might.

高适
（706–765）

燕歌行

汉家烟尘在东北，汉将辞家破残贼。
男儿本自重横行，天子非常赐颜色。
摐金伐鼓下榆关，旌旆逶迤碣石间。
校尉羽书飞瀚海，单于猎火照狼山。
山川萧条极边土，胡骑凭陵杂风雨。
战士军前半死生，美人帐下犹歌舞。
大漠穷秋塞草腓，孤城落日斗兵稀。
身当恩遇恒轻敌，力尽关山未解围。

In coats of mail they've served so long on the frontiers,
Since they left home their wives have shed streams of impearled tears.
In southern towns the women weep with broken heart;
In vain their men look southward, still they're far apart.
The northern front at stake, how can they go away?
On borders vast and desolate, how can they stay?
All day a cloud of slaughter mounts now and again;
All night the boom of gong is heard to chill the plain.
Each sees the other's sword bloodstained in the hard strife.
Will they care for reward when they give up their life?
Do you not know
The bitterness of fighting with the foe?
Can they forget the general sharing their weal and woe?

铁衣远戍辛勤久，玉箸应啼别离后。

少妇城南欲断肠，征人蓟北空回首。

边庭飘摇那可度，绝域苍茫更何有。

杀气三时作阵云，寒声一夜传刁斗。

相看白刃血纷纷，死节从来岂顾勋。

君不见沙场征战苦，至今犹忆李将军。

CHU GUANGXI
(707-c. 760)

The Fishing Bay

He comes to fish by lakeside green;
Late apricot blossoms run riot.
The pool seems shallow, for it's clean;
Fish go and leave lotus unquiet.
He waits for her by parting day;
And moors his boat at Willow Bay.

储光羲
（707– 约 760）

钓鱼湾

垂钓绿湾春，春深杏花乱。
潭清疑水浅，荷动知鱼散。
日暮待情人，维舟绿杨岸。

XU ANZHEN
(698-784)

My Neighbor's Lute

The Bear athwart the sky, the night is waxing deep,
I gaze upon the moon, too sad to fall asleep.
Suddenly from the bower I hear a lute is played,
I know it must be she, my neighbor's lovely maid.
The music sweet reminds me of her eyebrows fair;
Her fingers must be cold when lively turns the air.
But locked are her doors for the eyes indiscreet,
So I cannot see her but in the dreamland sweet.

徐安贞
（698–784）

闻邻家理筝

北斗横天夜欲阑，愁人倚月思无端。
忽闻画阁秦筝逸，知是邻家赵女弹。
曲成虚忆青蛾敛，调急遥怜玉指寒。
银锁重关听未辟，不如眠去梦中看。

ZHANG WEI
(711-777)

Early Mume Blossoms

Like white-jade belt against the cold mume flowers look,
Beside the pathway near the bridge over a brook.
If you don't know the streamside blossoms early blow,
You would take them for last winter's unmelted snow.

张渭
（711–777）

早梅

一树寒梅白玉条，
迥临村路傍溪桥。
不知近水花先发，
疑是经冬雪未销。

WAN CHU
(Dates Unknown)

A Dancer at Dragon-Boat Festival

Don't say the Western Beauty stands without a peer!
Today Green Jade rivals Flowers we revere.
Her eyebrows take the color of the verdant grass;
Her crimson skirt e'en pomegranate cannot surpass.
She sings a charming song and there's none but is charmed;
Her dance with captivating eyes makes all disarmed.
Who says the rainbow-hued threads can prolong our life?*
Tonight we'll give it up without an inner strife.

* It was believed that fivecolored threads wound around the arm on Dragon-Boat Festival, the fifth day of the fifth lunar month, could prolong life.

万楚
（生卒年不详）

五日观妓

西施谩道浣春纱，碧玉今时斗丽华。
眉黛夺将萱草色，红裙妒杀石榴花。
新歌一曲令人艳，醉舞双眸敛鬓斜。
谁道五丝能续命，却知今日死君家。

LIU CHANGQING
(709-780)

Seeking Shelter in Lotus Hill on a Snowy Night

At sunset hillside village still seems far;
Cold and deserted the thatched cottages are.
At wicket gate a dog is heard to bark;
With wind and snow I come when night is dark.

刘长卿
（709–780）

逢雪宿芙蓉山主人

日暮苍山远，

天寒白屋贫。

柴门闻犬吠，

风雪夜归人。

DU FU
(712-770)

Gazing at Mount Tai

O, peak of peaks, how high it stands!
One boundless green o'erspreads two states.
A marvel done by nature's hands,
O'er light and shade it dominates.
Clouds rise therefrom and lave my breast;
I strain my eyes and see birds fleet.
I must ascend the mountain's crest;
It dwarfs all peaks under my feet.

杜甫
（712–770）

望岳

岱宗夫如何？齐鲁青未了。
造化钟神秀，阴阳割昏晓。
荡胸生层云，决眦入归鸟。
会当凌绝顶，一览众山小。

Song of the Conscripts

Chariots rumble
And horses grumble.
The conscripts march with bow and arrows at the waist.
Their fathers, mothers, wives and children come in haste
To see them off; the bridge is shrouded in dust they've raised.
They clutch at the men's coats and stamp and bar the way;
Their grief cries loud and strikes the cloud straight, straightaway.
An onlooker by roadside asks an enrollee,
"The conscription is frequent," only answers he.
"Some went north at fifteen to guard the river shore
And were sent west to till the land at forty-four.
The elder bound their young heads when they went away;
Just home, they're sent to the frontier though their hair's grey.
The field on borderland becomes a sea of blood;
The emperor's greed for land is still at high flood.
Have you not heard two hundred districts east of the Hua Mountain lie
Where briers and brambles grow in villages far and nigh?
Although stout women can wield the plough and the hoe,
They know not east from west where thorns and weeds o'ergrow.
The enemy is used to hard and stubborn fight:
Our men are driven just like dogs or fowls in flight.

兵车行

车辚辚，马萧萧，行人弓箭各在腰。
耶娘妻子走相送，尘埃不见咸阳桥。
牵衣顿足拦道哭，哭声直上干云霄。
道旁过者问行人，行人但云点行频。
或从十五北防河，便至四十西营田。
去时里正与裹头，归来头白还戍边。
边庭流血成海水，武皇开边意未已。
君不闻汉家山东二百州，千村万落生荆杞。
纵有健妇把锄犁，禾生陇亩无东西。
况复秦兵耐苦战，被驱不异犬与鸡。

You are kind to ask me.
To complain I'm not free.
In winter of this year
Conscription goes on here.
The magistrates for taxes press;
How can we pay them in distress!
If we had known sons bring no joy,
We'd have preferred girl to boy.
A daughter can be married to a neighbor, alas!
A son can only be buried under the grass!
Have you not seen
On borders green
Bleached bones since olden days unburied on the plain?
The old ghosts weep and cry, while the new ghosts complain;
The air is loud with screech and scream in gloomy rain."

长者虽有问，役夫敢申恨？
且如今年冬，未休关西卒。
县官急索租，租税从何出？
信知生男恶，反是生女好。
生女犹得嫁比邻，生男埋没随百草。
君不见青海头，古来白骨无人收。
新鬼烦冤旧鬼哭，天阴雨湿声啾啾！

Spring View

On war-torn land streams flow and mountains stand;
In towns unquiet grass and weeds run riot.
Grieved o'er the years, flowers are moved to tears;
Seeing us part, birds cry with broken heart.
The beacon fire has gone higher and higher;
Words from household are worth their weight in gold.
I cannot bear to scratch my grizzling hair;
It grows too thin to hold a light hairpin.

春望

国破山河在，城春草木深。
感时花溅泪，恨别鸟惊心。
烽火连三月，家书抵万金。
白头搔更短，浑欲不胜簪。

The Pressgang at Stone Moat Village

I seek for shelter as night falls;
A pressgang comes and presses for more.
My poor old host climbs o'er the walls;
My hostess old answers the door.
How angry is the sergeant's shout!
How pitiful the woman's plight!
I hear what she tries to speak out:
"All my three sons have gone to fight,
And one of them sent word to me;
The other two in battle slain,
He'll keep alive if he can be;
The dead can't come to life again.
Within the house no man is left
Except my grandson at the breast;
His mother now of all bereft
Cannot come out, in tatters drest.
Though I'm a woman weak and old,
I beg to follow on your heels
That I may serve at the stronghold
And cook for you the morning meals."
With night her voices fade away;
I seem to hear still sob and sigh.
At dawn I go upon my way
And only bid my host good-bye.

石壕吏

暮投石壕村，有吏夜捉人。
老翁逾墙走，老妇出门看。
吏呼一何怒，妇啼一何苦！
听妇前致词:“三男邺城戍。
一男附书至，二男新战死。
存者且偷生，死者长已矣。
室中更无人，惟有乳下孙。
有孙母未去，出入无完裙。
老妪力虽衰，请从吏夜归。
急应河阳役，犹得备晨炊。”
夜久语声绝，如闻泣幽咽。
天明登前途，独与老翁别。

Written at Random (V)

The river's heartbroken to see spring pass away;
Standing on fragrant islet, I ask spring to stay.
But willow downs run wild and dance with wanton breeze;
Peach blossoms frivolous go with the stream at ease.

Welcome Rain on a Spring Night

Happy rain comes in time
When spring is in its prime.
With soft night breeze 'twill fall
And mutely moisten all.
Clouds darken river shore;
Lamps brighten all the more.
Saturated at dawn,
With flowers blooms the town.

漫兴（其五）

肠断春江欲尽头，杖藜徐步立芳洲。
颠狂柳絮随风舞，轻薄桃花逐水流。

春夜喜雨

好雨知时节，当春乃发生。
随风潜入夜，润物细无声。
野径云俱黑，江船火独明。
晓看红湿处，花重锦官城。

Recapture of the Regions North and South of the Yellow River

'Tis said the Northern Gate has been recaptured of late;
When the news reaches my ears, my gown is wet with tears.
Staring at my wife's face, of grief I find no trace;
As I roll up verse books, my joy like madness looks.
Though white-haired, I would still both sing and drink my fill;
With verdure spring's aglow; 'tis time we homeward go.
We shall sail all the way through Three Gorges in a day;
Going down to Xiangyang, we'll go up to Luoyang.

Ode to Autumn (I)

The pearl-like dewdrops wither maples in red dye;
The Gorge and Cliffs of Witch exhale dense fog around.
Up-surging river waves seem to storm the sky;
Dark clouds o'er mountains touch their shadows on the ground.
Twice full-blown, asters blown off draw tears from the eye;
Once tied up, lonely boats tie up my heart homebound.
Thinking of winter robes, everywhere tailors ply;
I hear at dusk but nearby washing blocks fast pound.

闻官军收河南河北

剑外忽传收蓟北，初闻涕泪满衣裳。
却看妻子愁何在，漫卷诗书喜欲狂。
白日放歌须纵酒，青春作伴好还乡。
即从巴峡穿巫峡，便下襄阳向洛阳。

秋兴八首（其一）

玉露凋伤枫树林，巫山巫峡气萧森。
江间波浪兼天涌，塞上风云接地阴。
丛菊两开他日泪，孤舟一系故园心。
寒衣处处催刀尺，白帝城高急暮砧。

On the Heights

The wind so swift and sky so wide, apes wail and cry;
Water so clear and beach so white, birds wheel and fly.
The boundless forest sheds its leaves shower by shower;
The endless river rolls its waves hour after hour.
A thousand miles from home, I'm grieved at autumn's plight;
Ill now and then for years, alone I'm on this height.
Living in times so hard, at frosted hair I pine;
Cast down by poverty, I have to give up wine.

Coming across Li Guinian* on the Southern Shore of the Yangtze River

How oft in princely mansions did we meet!
As oft in lordly halls I heard you sing.
The south with flowers is no longer sweet;
We chance to meet again in parting spring.

* A disfavored court musician.

登高

风急天高猿啸哀，渚清沙白鸟飞回。

无边落木萧萧下，不尽长江滚滚来。

万里悲秋常作客，百年多病独登台。

艰难苦恨繁霜鬓，潦倒新停浊酒杯。

江南逢李龟年

岐王宅里寻常见，崔九堂前几度闻。

正是江南好风景，落花时节又逢君。

CEN SHEN
(715-770)

Song of White Snow in Farewell to Secretary Wu, Going Back to the Capital

Snapping the pallid grass, the northern wind whirls low;
In the eighth moon the Tatar sky is filled with snow.
As if the vernal breeze had come back overnight,
Adorning thousands of pear trees with blossoms white.
Flakes enter pearled blinds and wet the silken screen;
No furs of fox can warm us nor brocade quilts green.
The general cannot draw his rigid bow with ease;
E'en the commissioner in coat of mail would freeze.
A thousand feet o'er cracked wilderness ice piles,
And gloomy clouds hang sad and drear for miles and miles.
We drink in headquarters to our guest homeward bound;
With Tatar lutes, pipas and pipes the camps resound.
Snow in large flakes at dusk falls heavy on camp gate;
The frozen red flag in the wind won't undulate.
At eastern gate of Wheel Tower we bid good-bye
On the snow-covered road to Heaven's Mountain high.
I watch his horse go past a bend and, lost to sight,
His track will soon be covered by the snow in flight.

岑参
（715–770）

白雪歌送武判官归京

北风卷地白草折，胡天八月即飞雪。
忽如一夜春风来，千树万树梨花开。
散入珠帘湿罗幕，狐裘不暖锦衾薄。
将军角弓不得控，都护铁衣冷难着。
瀚海阑干百丈冰，愁云惨淡万里凝。
中军置酒饮归客，胡琴琵琶与羌笛。
纷纷暮雪下辕门，风掣红旗冻不翻。
轮台东门送君去，去时雪满天山路。
山回路转不见君，雪上空留马行处。

Song of Running-Horse River in Farewell to General Feng on His Western Expedition

Do you not see Running-Horse River flow
Along the sea of snow
And sand that's yellowed sky and earth and high and low?
In the ninth moon at Wheel Tower winds howl at night;
The river fills with boulders fallen from the height;
With howling winds they run riot as if in flight.
When grass turns yellow and plump Hunnish horses neigh,
West of Mount Gold dusts rise, the foe in proud array.
Our general leads his army on his westward way.
He keeps his iron amour on the whole night long;
Spears clang at midnight when his army march along,
Their faces cut by winds that blow so sharp and strong.
Both snow and sweat turn into steam on horse's mane,
Which soon on horse's back turns into ice again.
Ink freezes when the challenge's writ before campaign.
On hearing this, the foe with fear should palpitate.
Dare they cross swords with our brave men in iron plate?
We'll wait for news of victory at the western gate.

走马川行奉送出师西征

君不见走马川，雪海边，
平沙莽莽黄入天。
轮台九月风夜吼，一川碎石大如斗，
随风满地石乱走。
匈奴草黄马正肥，金山西见烟尘飞，
汉家大将西出师。
将军金甲夜不脱，半夜军行戈相拨，
风头如刀面如割。
马毛带雪汗气蒸，五花连钱旋作冰，
幕中草檄砚水凝。
虏骑闻之应胆慑，料知短兵不敢接，
车师西门伫献捷。

LIU FANGPING
(Dates Unknown)

A Moonlit Night

The moon has brightened half the house at dead of night;
The slanting Plough and Southern stars shed dying light.
I feel the warmth of air exhaled by coming spring
As through my window screen I hear the insects sing.

刘方平
（生卒年不详）

月夜

更深月色半人家，
北斗阑干南斗斜。
今夜偏知春气暖，
虫声新透绿窗纱。

YANG YUHUAN
(719-756)*

Dancing

Silk sleeves are swaying ceaselessly with fragrance spread;
In autumn mist are floating lotus lilies red.
Light clouds o'er mountains high ripple with breezes cool;
Young willow shoots caress water of garden pool.

* The beautiful mistress of Emperor Xuan Zong of the Tang Dynasty. See Bai Juyi's long poem "The Everlasting Regret."

杨玉环
（719–756）

赠张云容舞

罗袖动香香不已，
红蕖袅袅秋烟里。
轻云岭上乍摇风，
嫩柳池边初拂水。

YUAN JIE
(719-772)

Drinking Song on Stone Fish Lake*

On stone Fish Lake as on Dongting I gaze my fill,
On brimming summer water as on verdant hill.
Using the vale as cup and water as wine pools,
The tipplers sit on rocks as cozy as on stools.
The wind so strong has formed great waves from day to day;
It can't prevent the boats from bringing wine this way.
A ladle in my hand, I sit on rocky shore;
To do away with care, all drink the wine I pour.

* The lake got its name from a fish-shaped rock. The poet stored wine in the rock's concavities.

元结
（719–772）

石鱼湖上醉歌

石鱼湖，似洞庭，夏水欲满君山青。
山为樽，水为沼，酒徒历历坐洲岛。
长风连日作大浪，不能废人运酒舫。
我持长瓢坐巴丘，酌饮四坐以散愁。

ZHANG JI
(c. 715-779)

Mooring near Maple Bridge at Night

The moon goes down, crows cry under a frosty sky,
Dimly lit fishing boats 'neath maples sadly lie.
Beyond the Suzhou walls the Temple of Cold Hill
Rings bells, which reach my boat, breaking the midnight still.

张继

（约 715–779）

枫桥夜泊

月落乌啼霜满天，
江枫渔火对愁眠。
姑苏城外寒山寺，
夜半钟声到客船。

QIAN QI
(722-780)

To the Returning Wild Geese

Wild geese, why don't you stay there any more,
Where water's blue, sand bright and mossy shore?
The moonbeams play on twenty-five sad strings.*
Can you not bear the grief the zither brings?

* Legend said that the Goddess of River Xiang by moonlight played the twenty-five-stringed zither in mourning for her husband, Emperor Shen, buried at the foot of the southern hill.

钱起
（722–780）

归雁

潇湘何事等闲回？
水碧沙明两岸苔。
二十五弦弹夜月，
不胜清怨却飞来。

JIA ZHI
(718-772)

Spring Thoughts

The yellow willows wave above, green grass below;
Peach blooms run riot and plum blossoms fragrant grow.
The vernal wind can never blow my grief away;
My woe increases with each lengthening spring day.

贾至
（718–772）

春思

草色青青柳色黄，
桃花历乱李花香。
东风不为吹愁去，
春日偏能惹恨长。

HAN HONG
(Dates Unknown)

Cold-Food Day*

Nowhere in vernal town but sweet flowers fly down;
Riverside willow trees slant in the eastern breeze.
At dusk the palace sends privilege candles red
To lordly houses, where wreaths of smoke rise and spread.

* Cold-Food Day marked the end of the three-day period when Chinese families refrained from starting cooking fires at home. It was also the season when they visited their ancestral burial mounds.

韩翃
（生卒年不详）

寒食

春城无处不飞花，
寒食东风御柳斜。
日暮汉宫传蜡烛，
轻烟散入五侯家。

SIKONG SHU
(720-790)

Farewell to a Friend

Although I know that we shall meet again,
How can we bear on such a night to part?
Do you think wine and friendship can retain
No longer than an adverse wind your heart?

司空曙
（720–790）

别卢秦卿

知有前期在，
难分此夜中。
无将故人酒，
不及石尤风。

ZHANG ZHIHE
(730-810)

Tune: "A Fisherman's Song"

In front of western hills white egrets fly up and down
Over peach-mirrored stream, where perches are full grown.
In my broad-brimmed blue hat
And green straw cloak, I'd fain
Go fishing, careless of the slanting wind and rain.

张志和
（730–810）

渔歌子

西塞山前白鹭飞，
桃花流水鳜鱼肥。
青箬笠，绿蓑衣，
斜风细雨不须归。

DAI SHULUN
(732-789)

Tune: "Song of Flirtation"

Borderland grass,
Borderland grass,
It withers up and men grow old, alas!
The south and north of mountains bright with snow,
For miles and miles bright moonbeams flow.
Bright is the moon,
Bright is the moon,
Men die of grief on hearing Hunnish tune.

戴叔伦

（732–789）

调笑令・边草

边草，边草，边草尽来兵老。

山南山北雪晴，千里万里月明。

明月，明月，胡笳一声愁绝。

LI DUAN
(737-784)

The Zitherist

How clear the golden zither rings
When her fair fingers touch its strings!
To draw attention from her lord,
Now and then she strikes a discord.

李端

（737–784）

鸣筝

鸣筝金粟柱，

素手玉房前。

欲得周郎顾，

时时误拂弦。

WEI YINGWU
(737-789)

On the West Stream at Chuzhou

Alone, I like the riverside where green grass grows
And golden orioles sing amid the leafy trees.
When showers fall at dusk, the river overflows;
A lonely boat athwart the ferry floats at ease.

Tune: "Song of Flirtation"

The Hunnish steed,
The Hunnish steed,
Far away at the foot of Mount Rouge it will feed.
Now through sand, now through snow, it will gallop and neigh.
Looking east, looking west, it's lost its backward way.
Its way is lost,
Its way is lost,
The boundless grassland with the setting sun's embossed.

韦应物
（737–789）

滁州西涧

独怜幽草涧边生，上有黄鹂深树鸣。
春潮带雨晚来急，野渡无人舟自横。

调笑令·胡马

胡马，胡马，远放燕支山下。
跑沙跑雪独嘶，东望西望路迷。
迷路，迷路，边草无穷日暮。

LU LUN
(c. 748-c. 800)

Grief in Autumn

As years pass by, grey grows my hair;
When autumn's come, the trees stand bare.
Perplexed, I ask the yellow leaf,
"Do you like me feel gnawed by grief?"

卢纶
（约 748– 约 800）

伤秋

岁去人头白，
秋来树叶黄。
搔头向黄叶，
与尔共悲伤。

LI YI
(748-827)

On Hearing a Flute at Night atop the Victor's Wall

Below the beacon tower sand looks white as snow;
Beyond the Victor's Wall like frost cold moonbeams flow.
None knows from where a flute blows a nostalgic song;
All warriors lie awake homesick the whole night long.

李益
（748–827）

夜上受降城闻笛

回乐峰前沙似雪，
受降城外月如霜。
不知何处吹芦管，
一夜征人尽望乡。

LYRICS FROM DUNHUANG

Tune: "Buddhist Dancers"

On the pillow we make a thousand vows; we say
Our love will last unless green mountains rot away,
On the water can float a lump of lead,
The Yellow River dries up to the bed,
Stars can be seen in broad daylight,
The Dipper in the south shines bright.
E'en so, our love will not be done
Unless at midnight rise the sun.

敦煌曲子词

菩萨蛮

枕前发尽千般愿，要休且待青山烂。
水面上秤锤浮，直待黄河彻底枯。
白日参辰现，北斗回南面。
休即未能休，且待三更见日头。

Tune: “The Magpie on a Branch”

How can I bear to hear the chattering magpie
Announce happy news on which I can’t rely?
So thus I catch it live when it flies to me again
And shut it in a cage, where lonely ’twill remain.

With good intent I brought her a happy message.
Who would expect she’d shut me in a golden cage?
I wish her husband would come back soon, so that I
Might be set free and take my flight to the blue sky.

鹊踏枝

叵耐灵鹊多谩语，送喜何曾有凭据？
几度飞来活捉取，锁上金笼休共语。

比拟好心来送喜，谁知锁我在金笼里。
欲他征夫早归来，腾身却放我向青云里。

Tune: "Silk-Washing Stream"

After we pass the five-mile beach, the breeze stops blowing;
With sails unfurled, the boat seems light when we are rowing.
We use no scull and take our oars from water flowing,
But still the boat is going.

The water shimmers in the breeze before the eye;
As if to bid us welcome, the mountain comes nigh;
On a close look it does not move but towers high;
The boat is going by.

浣溪沙

五两竿头风欲平，长风举棹觉船轻。
柔橹不施停却棹，是船行。
满眼风波多闪烁，看山恰似走来迎。
仔细看山山不动，是船行。

MENG JIAO
(751-814)

Song of the Parting Son

The thread in the mom's hand–
A gown for the parting son.
Sewn stitch by stitch before he goes away
So the coldness of the winds he might stand.
As the grass can give naught to the sun
Neither the son the loving mom repay.

Successful at the Civil Service Exam

Gone are all my past woes! What more have I to say?
My body and my mind enjoy their fill today.
Successful, my horse runs faster in vernal breeze;
I've seen within one day all flowers on Chang'an trees.

孟郊

（751–814）

游子吟

慈母手中线，游子身上衣。
临行密密缝，意恐迟迟归。
谁言寸草心，报得三春晖。

登科后

昔日龌龊不足夸，今朝放荡思无涯。
春风得意马蹄疾，一日看尽长安花。

CUI HU
(772-846)

Written in a Village South of the Capital

This very day last year, oh, at this very place,
A pretty face outshone the flowers of peach trees.
I do not know today where shines the pretty face;
Only the pretty flowers smile in vernal breeze.

崔护

（772–846）

题都城南庄

去年今日此门中，
人面桃花相映红。
人面不知何处去，
桃花依旧笑春风。

RONG YU
(744-800)

Leaving the Lakeside Pavilion While Moving House

I love the lakeside pavilion in vernal breeze;
My sleeves are twined by twigs of weeping willow trees.
The orioles there nesting seem to know my heart;
They utter cry on cry before I part.

戎昱
（744–800）

移家别湖上亭

好是春风湖上亭，
柳条藤蔓系离情。
黄莺久住浑相识，
欲别频啼四五声。

ZHANG JI
(c. 768-830)

Reply of a Chaste Wife

You know I love my husband best,
Yet two bright pearls are sent me still.
I hung them in my red silk vest,
So grateful I'm for your good will.
You see my house o'erlooking gardens and
My husband guards the place, halberd in hand.
I know your heart as noble as the sun in the skies,
But I have sworn to serve my husband all my life.
With your twin pearls I send back two tears from my eyes.
Would we had met before I was a wife!

张籍

（约 768–830）

节妇吟

君知妾有夫，赠妾双明珠。

感君缠绵意，系在红罗襦。

妾家高楼连苑起，良人执戟明光里。

知君用心如日月，事夫誓拟同生死。

还君明珠双泪垂，恨不相逢未嫁时。

WANG JIAN
(768-c. 833)

Waiting for Her Husband

Waiting for him alone
Where the river goes by,
She turns into a stone
Gazing with longing eye.
Atop the hill from day to day come wind and rain;
The stone should speak to see her husband come again.

Tune: "Song of Flirtation"

The willows stand,
The willows stand
At dusk at Ferry of White Sand.
The brimming river waves seen at the prow would make
The heart of merchant's young wife break.
'Twould break her heart,
'Twould break her heart,
To see at night a pair of partridges fly apart.

王建
（768– 约 833）

望夫石

望夫处，江悠悠。
化为石，不回头。
上头日日风复雨，
行人归来石应语。

调笑令 · 杨柳

杨柳，杨柳，日暮白沙渡口。
船头江水茫茫，商人少妇断肠。
肠断，肠断，鹧鸪夜飞失伴。

HAN YU
(768-824)

Written for My Grandnephew at the Blue Pass

To the Celestial Court a proposal was made,
And I am banished eight thousand miles away.
To undo the misdeeds I would have given aid.
Would I have dared spare myself with powers in decay?
The ridge veiled in barred clouds, my home cannot be seen;
The Blue Pass covered by snow, my horse won't forward go.
You have come from afar and I know what you mean;
Not to leave my bones there where misty waters flow.

韩愈

（768–824）

左迁至蓝关示侄孙湘

一封朝奏九重天，夕贬潮州路八千。
欲为圣明除弊事，肯将衰朽惜残年！
云横秦岭家何在？雪拥蓝关马不前。
知汝远来应有意，好收吾骨瘴江边。

ZHANG ZHONGSU
(769-819)

In Reverie

By city wall wave willows slender
And roadside mulberry leaves tender.
She gathers not, basket in hand,
Still dreaming of the far-off land.

The Pavilion of Swallows* (I)

Upstairs the dying lamp flickers with morning frost;
The lonely widow rises from her nuptial bed.
Sleepless the whole night long, in mournful thoughts she's lost;
The night seems endless as the boundless sky o'erhead.

* The Pavilion of Swallows in Pengcheng (present-day Xuzhou) was where the fair lady Panpan, famous singer and dancer of the Tang Dynasty, lived alone for ten years, refusing to remarry after the death of her beloved lord, who was a friend of Zhang Zhongsu and Bai Juyi.

张仲素

（769–819）

春闺思

袅袅城边柳，青青陌上桑。

提笼忘采叶，昨夜梦渔阳。

燕子楼（其一）

楼上残灯伴晓霜，独眠人起合欢床。

相思一夜情多少，地角天涯未是长。

The Pavilion of Swallows (II)

The pine before his grave is shrouded in sad smoke;
In the Swallows' Pavilion pensive she appears.
Her songs are hushed, for buried are his sword and cloak;
Her dancing dress has lost its perfume for ten years.

The Pavilion of Swallows (III)

She's seen wild geese from her lord's grave on backward way,
And now she sees the swallows come with spring again.
On flute and zither she is in no mood to play;
Buried in spider's webs and dusty they remain.

燕子楼（其二）

北邙松柏锁愁烟，燕子楼中思悄然。
自埋剑履歌尘散，红袖香销已十年。

燕子楼（其三）

适看鸿雁洛阳回，又睹玄禽逼社来。
瑶瑟玉箫无意绪，任从蛛网任从灰。

LIU YUXI
(772-842)

Reply to Bai Juyi, Whom I Meet for the First Time at a Banquet in Yangzhou

Oh, western mountains and southern streams desolate,
Where I, an exile, lived for twenty years and three!
To mourn for my departed friends I come too late;
In native land I look like human debris.
A thousand sails pass by the side of sunken ship;
Ten thousand flowers bloom ahead of injured tree.
Today I hear you chant the praise of comradeship;
I wish this cup of wine might well inspirit me.

The Autumn Breeze

From where arose the autumn breeze?
It sends wild geese off sad and drear.
At dawn it enters courtyard trees;
The lonely one's the first to hear.

刘禹锡

（772–842）

酬乐天扬州初逢席上见赠

巴山楚水凄凉地，二十三年弃置身。

怀旧空吟闻笛赋，到乡翻似烂柯人。

沉舟侧畔千帆过，病树前头万木春。

今日听君歌一曲，暂凭杯酒长精神。

秋风引

何处秋风至？萧萧送雁群。

朝来入庭树，孤客最先闻。

Tune: "Bamboo-Branch Song" (I)

Between the willows green the river flows along;
My dear one in a boat is heard to sing a song.
The west is veiled in rain, the east enjoys sunshine;
My dear one is as deep in love as day is fine.

Tune: "Bamboo-Branch Song" (II)

The mountain's red with peach blossoms above;
The shore is washed by spring water below;
Red blossoms fade as fast as my gallant's love,
The river like my sorrow will ever flow.

竹枝词二首（其一）

杨柳青青江水平，闻郎江上踏歌声。

东边日出西边雨，道是无晴却有晴。

竹枝词九首（其二）

山桃红花满上头，蜀江春水拍山流。

花红易衰似郎意，水流无限似侬愁。

Tune: "Ripples Sifting Sand"

The sun dispels the mist and shines on river strand;
The crook is crowded with women washing gold from sand.
The seals of kings and lords, trinkets of ladies fair
Are taken from the sand by these women with care.

Drinking Before Peonies in Bloom

Today I'll drink with blooms before.
Don't mind if I drink two cups more.
I am afraid lest to be told,
"Our bloom is not for you, the old!"*

浪淘沙

日照澄洲江雾开，淘金女伴满江隈。
美人首饰侯王印，尽是沙中浪底来。

饮酒看牡丹

今日花前饮，甘心醉数杯。
但愁花有语，不为老人开。

BAI JUYI
(772-846)

The White-Haired Palace Maid

The Shangyang Palace maid,
Her hair grows white, her rosy cheeks grow dark and fade.
The palace gate is guarded by eunuchs in green.*
How many springs have passed, immured as she has been!
She was first chosen for the imperial household
At the age of sixteen; now she's sixty years old.
The hundred beauties brought in with her have all gone,
Flickering out through long years, leaving her alone.*
She swallowed grief when she left home in days gone by;
They helped her into the cab, forbidding her to cry.
Once in the palace, she would be favored, they said;
Her face was fair as lotus, her bosom like jade.*
But to the emperor she could never come nigh;
The Lady Yang had cast on her a jealous eye.*
She was consigned to Shangyang Palace full of gloom,
To pass her remaining days in a lonely room.
In empty chamber long seemed each autumnal night;
Sleepless in bed, it seemed she'd never see daylight.
Dim, dim the lamplight throws her shadow on the walls;
Shower by shower on her window chill rain falls.
Spring days drag slow;
She sits alone to see light won't be dim and low.
She's tired to hear the palace orioles sing and sing,
Too old to envy pairs of swallows on the wing.

白居易

（772–846）

上阳白发人

上阳人，红颜暗老白发新。
绿衣监使守宫门，一闭上阳多少春。
玄宗末岁初选入，入时十六今六十。
同时采择百余人，零落年深残此身。
忆昔吞悲别亲族，扶入车中不教哭。
皆云入内便承恩，脸似芙蓉胸似玉。
未容君王得见面，已被杨妃遥侧目。
妒令潜配上阳宫，一生遂向空房宿。
宿空房，秋夜长，夜长无寐天不明。
耿耿残灯背壁影，萧萧暗雨打窗声。
春日迟，日迟独坐天难暮。
宫莺百啭愁厌闻，梁燕双栖老休妒。

Silent, she sees the birds appear and disappear
And counts nor springs nor autumns coming year by year.
Watching the moon o'er palace again and again,
Four hundred times and more she's seen it wax and wane.*
Today the oldest honorable maid of all,
She is entitled Secretary of Palace Hall.
Her gown is tightly fitted, her shoes like pointed prows;
With dark pencil she draws long, slender brows.*
Seeing her, people outside would e'en laugh with tears,
For her old-fashioned dress has been out of date for years.
The Shangyang maid, to suffer is her privilege;
She suffered while still young, she suffers in old age.
Do you not know a satire spread in days gone by?
Today for white-haired Shangyang Palace maid we'll sigh!

* Yang Xianyi's translation versified.

莺归燕去长悄然，春往秋来不记年。

唯向深宫望明月，东西四五百回圆。

今日宫中年最老，大家遥赐尚书号。

小头鞋履窄衣裳，青黛点眉眉细长。

外人不见见应笑，天宝末年时世妆。

上阳人，苦最多。

少亦苦，老亦苦，少苦老苦两如何？

君不见昔时吕向美人赋，

又不见今日上阳白发歌！

The Old Charcoal Seller*

What's the old man's affair?
He cuts the wood in southern hills and fires his ware.
His face is grimed with smoke and streaked with ash and dust,
His temples grizzled and his fingers all turned black.
The money made by selling charcoal is not just
Enough for food and clothing for his mouth and back.
Although his coat is thin, he hopes winter will set in,
For weather cold will keep up the charcoal's good price.
At night a foot of snow falls outside the city walls;
At dawn his charcoal cart crushes ruts in the ice.
The sun is high, the ox tired out and hungry he,
Outside the southern gate in snow and slush they rest.
Two riders canter up; alas! Who can they be?
Two palace heralds in the yellow jackets dressed.
Decree in hand, which is imperial order, one says;
They turn the cart about and at the ox they shout.
A cartload of charcoal a thousand catties weighs;
They drive the cart away. What dare the old man say!
Ten feet of silk and twenty feet of gauze deep red–
That is the payment they fasten to the ox's head.

---

* Yang Xianyi's translation versified.

卖炭翁

卖炭翁，伐薪烧炭南山中。
满面尘灰烟火色，两鬓苍苍十指黑。
卖炭得钱何所营？身上衣裳口中食。
可怜身上衣正单，心忧炭贱愿天寒。
夜来城外一尺雪，晓驾炭车辗冰辙。
牛困人饥日已高，市南门外泥中歇。
翩翩两骑来是谁？黄衣使者白衫儿。
手把文书口称敕，回车叱牛牵向北。
一车炭，千余斤，宫使驱将惜不得。
半匹红纱一丈绫，系向牛头充炭直。

The Everlasting Regret

The beauty-loving monarch longed year after year
To find a beautiful lady without peer.
A maiden of the Yangs* to womanhood just grown,
In inner chambers bred, to the world was unknown.
Endowed with natural beauty too hard to hide,
One day she stood selected for the monarch's side.
Turning her head, she smiled so sweet and full of grace
That she outshone in six palaces the fairest face.
She bathed in glassy water of warm-fountain pool,
Which laved and smoothed her creamy skin when spring was cool.
Upborne by her attendants, she rose too faint to move,
And this was when she first received the monarch's love.
Flowerlike face and cloudlike hair, golden-headdressed,
In lotus-flower curtain she spent the night blessed.
She slept till sun rose high, for the blessed night was short;
From then on the monarch held no longer morning court.
In revels as in feasts she shared her lord's delight,
His companion on trips and his mistress at night.
In inner palace dwelt three thousand ladies fair;
On her alone was lavished royal love and care.
Her beauty served the night when dressed in Golden Bower
Or drunk with wine and spring at banquet in Jade Tower.
All her sisters and brothers received rank and fief
And honors showered on her household, to the grief
Of the fathers and mothers who'd rather give birth

---

* Yang Yuhuan (719-756) was the favorite mistress of Emperor Xuan Zong (r. 725-768) of the Tang Dynasty.

长恨歌

汉皇重色思倾国，御宇多年求不得。
杨家有女初长成，养在深闺人未识。
天生丽质难自弃，一朝选在君王侧。
回眸一笑百媚生，六宫粉黛无颜色。
春寒赐浴华清池，温泉水滑洗凝脂。
侍儿扶起娇无力，始是新承恩泽时。
云鬓花颜金步摇，芙蓉帐暖度春宵。
春宵苦短日高起，从此君王不早朝。
承欢侍宴无闲暇，春从春游夜专夜。
后宫佳丽三千人，三千宠爱在一身。
金屋妆成娇侍夜，玉楼宴罢醉和春。
姊妹弟兄皆列土，可怜光彩生门户。
遂令天下父母心，不重生男重生女。

To a fair maiden than any son on earth.
The lofty palace towered high into blue cloud,
With wind-borne music so divine the air was loud.
Seeing slow dance and hearing fluted or stringed song,
The emperor was never tired the whole day long.

But rebels* beat their war drums, making the earth quake
And "Song of Rainbow Skirt and Coat of Feathers" break.
A cloud of dust was raised o'er city walls nine-fold;
Thousands of chariots and horsemen southwestward rolled.
Imperial flags moved slowly now and halted then,
And thirty miles from Western Gate they stopped again.
Six armies would not march–what could be done? –with speed
Until the Lady Yang was killed before the steed.
None would pick up her hairpin fallen to the ground
Or golden bird and comb with which her head was crowned.
The monarch could not save her and hid his face in fear;
Turning his head, he saw her blood mix with his tear.
The yellow dust spread wide, the wind blew desolate;
A serpentine plank path led to cloud-capped Sword Gate.
Below the Eyebrow Mountains wayfarers were few;
In fading sunlight royal standards lost their hue.
On western waters blue and western mountains green
The monarch's heart was daily gnawed by sorrow keen.
The moon viewed from his tent shed a soul-searing light;
The bells heard in night rain made a heart-rending sound.

Suddenly the tide turned. Returning from his flight,
The monarch could not tear himself away from the ground
Where 'mid the clods beneath the slope he couldn't forget
The fair-faced Lady Yang, who was unfairly slain.

---

* The revolt broke out in 755 and forced the emperor to flee from the capital.

骊宫高处入青云，仙乐风飘处处闻。
缓歌慢舞凝丝竹，尽日君王看不足。
渔阳鼙鼓动地来，惊破霓裳羽衣曲。
九重城阙烟尘生，千乘万骑西南行。
翠华摇摇行复止，西出都门百余里。
六军不发无奈何，宛转蛾眉马前死。
花钿委地无人收，翠翘金雀玉搔头。
君王掩面救不得，回看血泪相和流。
黄埃散漫风萧索，云栈萦纡登剑阁。
峨嵋山下少人行，旌旗无光日色薄。
蜀江水碧蜀山青，圣主朝朝暮暮情。
行宫见月伤心色，夜雨闻铃肠断声。
天旋地转回龙驭，到此踌躇不能去。
马嵬坡下泥土中，不见玉颜空死处。

He looked at the ministers, with tears their robes were wet;
They rode east to the capital, but with loose rein.
Back, he found her pond and garden in the old place,
With lotus in the lake and willows by the hall.
Willow leaves resembled her brows and lotus her face;
At the sight of all these, how could his tears not fall
Or when in vernal breeze were peach and plum full-blown
Or when in autumn rain parasol leaves were shed?
In western as in southern court was grass o'ergrown;
With fallen leaves unswept the marble steps turned red.
Actors, although still young, began to have hair grey;
Eunuchs and waiting maids looked old in palace deep.
Fireflies flitting the hall, mutely he pined away;
The lonely lampwick burned out; still he could not sleep.
Slowly beat drums and rang bells; night began to grow long;
Bright shone the Milky Way; daybreak seemed to come late.
The lovebird tiles grew chilly with hoar frost so strong,
And his kingfisher quilt was cold, not shared by a mate.
One long, long year the dead and the living were parted;
Her soul came not in dreams to see the brokenhearted.

A Taoist sorcerer came to the palace door,
Skilled to summon the spirit from the other shore.
Moved by the monarch's yearning for the departed fair,
He was ordered to seek for her everywhere.
Borne on the air, like a flash of lightning he flew;
In heaven and on earth he searched through and through.
Up to the azure vault and down to deepest place,
Nor above nor below could he e'er find her trace.
He learned that on the sea were fairy mountains proud
That now appeared, now disappeared amid the cloud
Of rainbow colors where rose magnificent bowers
And dwelt so many fairies as graceful as flowers.

君臣相顾尽沾衣，东望都门信马归。
归来池苑皆依旧，太液芙蓉未央柳。
芙蓉如面柳如眉，对此如何不泪垂。
春风桃李花开日，秋雨梧桐叶落时。
西宫南内多秋草，落叶满阶红不扫。
梨园弟子白发新，椒房阿监青娥老。
夕殿萤飞思悄然，孤灯挑尽未成眠。
迟迟钟鼓初长夜，耿耿星河欲曙天。
鸳鸯瓦冷霜华重，翡翠衾寒谁与共。
悠悠生死别经年，魂魄不曾来入梦。
临邛道士鸿都客，能以精诚致魂魄。
为感君王辗转思，遂教方士殷勤觅。
排空驭气奔如电，升天入地求之遍。
上穷碧落下黄泉，两处茫茫皆不见。
忽闻海上有仙山，山在虚无缥缈间。
楼阁玲珑五云起，其中绰约多仙子。

Among them was a queen whose name was Ever True;
Her snow-white skin and sweet face might afford a clue.
Knocking at western gate of palace hall, he bade
The porter fair to inform the queen's waiting maid.
When she heard there came the monarch's embassy,
The queen was startled out of dreams in her canopy.
Pushing aside the pillow, she rose and got dressed,
Passing through silver screen and pearl shade to meet the guest.
Her cloudlike hair awry, not full awake at all,
Her flowery cap slanted, she came into the hall.
The wind blew up her fairy sleeves and made them float
As if she danced the "Rainbow Skirt and Feathered Coat."
Her jade-white face crisscrossed with tears in lonely world
Like a spray of pear blossoms in spring rain impearled.
She bade him thank her lord, lovesick and brokenhearted;
They knew nothing of each other after they parted.
Love and happiness long ended within palace walls;
Days and months appeared long in the fairyland halls.
Turning her head and fixing on the earth her gaze,
She saw no capital 'mid clouds of dust and haze.
To show her love was deep, she took out keepsakes old
For him to carry back, hairpin and case of gold.
Keeping one side of the case and one wing of the pin,
She sent to her dear lord the other half of the twin.
"If our two hearts as firm as the gold should remain,
In heaven or on earth we'll sometime meet again."
At parting she confided to the messenger
A secret vow known only to her lord and her.
On seventh day of seventh moon when none was near,
At midnight in Long Life Hall he whispered in her ear,
"On high, we'd be two lovebirds flying wing to wing;
On earth, two trees with branches twined from spring to spring."
The boundless sky and endless earth may pass away,
But this vow unfulfilled will be regretted for aye.

中有一人字太真，雪肤花貌参差是。
金阙西厢叩玉扃，转教小玉报双成。
闻道汉家天子使，九华帐里梦魂惊。
揽衣推枕起徘徊，珠箔银屏迤逦开。
云鬓半偏新睡觉，花冠不整下堂来。
风吹仙袂飘飖举，犹似霓裳羽衣舞。
玉容寂寞泪阑干，梨花一枝春带雨。
含情凝睇谢君王，一别音容两渺茫。
昭阳殿里恩爱绝，蓬莱宫中日月长。
回头下望人寰处，不见长安见尘雾。
唯将旧物表深情，钿合金钗寄将去。
钗留一股合一扇，钗擘黄金合分钿。
但教心似金钿坚，天上人间会相见。
临别殷勤重寄词，词中有誓两心知。
七月七日长生殿，夜半无人私语时。
在天愿作比翼鸟，在地愿为连理枝。
天长地久有时尽，此恨绵绵无绝期。

Song of a Pipa Player

One night by riverside I bade a friend good-bye;
In maple leaves and rushes autumn seemed to sigh.
My friend and I dismounted and came into the boat;
We wished to drink but there was no music afloat.
Without flute songs we drank our cups with heavy heart;
The moonbeams blent with water when we were to part.
Suddenly o'er the stream we heard a pipa sound;
I forgot to go home and the guest stood spellbound.
We followed where the music led to find the player,
But heard the pipa stop and no music in the air.
We moved our boat beside the player's to invite
Her to drink at replenished feast by lamplight.
Again we called and urged her to appear until
She came, her face half hid behind a pipa still.
She turned the pegs and tested twice or thrice each string;
Before a tune was played we heard her feelings sing.
Then note on note she struck with pathos deep and strong;
It seemed to say she'd missed her dreams all her life long.
Head bent, she played with unpremeditated art
On and on to pour out her overflowing heart.
She lightly plucked, slowly stroked and twanged loud
The song of "Green Waist" after that of "Rainbow Cloud."
The thick strings loudly thrummed like the pattering rain;
The fine strings softly tinkled in murmuring strain.
When mingling loud and soft notes were together played,
'Twas like large and small pearls dropping on plate of jade.

琵琶行

浔阳江头夜送客，枫叶荻花秋瑟瑟。
主人下马客在船，举酒欲饮无管弦。
醉不成欢惨将别，别时茫茫江浸月。
忽闻水上琵琶声，主人忘归客不发。
寻声暗问弹者谁？琵琶声停欲语迟。
移船相近邀相见，添酒回灯重开宴。
千呼万唤始出来，犹抱琵琶半遮面。
转轴拨弦三两声，未成曲调先有情。
弦弦掩抑声声思，似诉平生不得志。
低眉信手续续弹，说尽心中无限事。
轻拢慢捻抹复挑，初为霓裳后六幺。
大弦嘈嘈如急雨，小弦切切如私语。
嘈嘈切切错杂弹，大珠小珠落玉盘。

Now clear like orioles warbling in flowery land,
Then sobbing like a stream running along the sand.
But the stream seemed so cold as to tighten the string;
From tightened strings no more sound could be heard to ring.
Still we heard hidden grief and vague regret concealed;
Music expressed then far less than silence revealed.
Suddenly we heard water burst a silver jar,
The clash of spears and sabres coming from afar.
She made a central sweep when the music was ending;
The four strings made one sound, as of silk one is rending.
Silence reigned left and right of the boat, east and west;
We saw but autumn moon white in the river's breast.

She slid the plectrum pensively between the strings,
Smoothed out her dress and rose with a composed mien.
"I spent," she said, "in capital my early springs,
Where at the foot of Mount of Toads my home had been.
At thirteen I learned on the pipa how to play,
And my name was among the primas of the day.
My skill the admiration of the masters won,
And my beauty was envied by deserted fair one.
The gallant young men vied to shower gifts on me;
One tune played, countless silk rolls were given with glee.
Beating time, I let silver comb and pin drop down,
And spilt-out wine oft stained my blood-red silken gown.
From year to year I laughed my joyous life away
On moonlit autumn night or windy vernal day.
My younger brother left for war, and died my maid;
Days passed, nights came, and my beauty began to fade.
Fewer and fewer were cabs and steeds at my door;
I married a smug merchant when my prime was o'er.

间关莺语花底滑，幽咽泉流冰下难。
冰泉冷涩弦凝绝，凝绝不通声暂歇。
别有幽愁暗恨生，此时无声胜有声。
银瓶乍破水浆迸，铁骑突出刀枪鸣。
曲终收拨当心画，四弦一声如裂帛。
东船西舫悄无言，唯见江心秋月白。

沉吟放拨插弦中，整顿衣裳起敛容。
自言本是京城女，家在虾蟆陵下住。
十三学得琵琶成，名属教坊第一部。
曲罢曾教善才服，妆成每被秋娘妒。
五陵年少争缠头，一曲红绡不知数。
钿头银篦击节碎，血色罗裙翻酒污。
今年欢笑复明年，秋月春风等闲度。
弟走从军阿姨死，暮去朝来颜色故。
门前冷落鞍马稀，老大嫁作商人妇。

The merchant cared for money much more than for me;
One month ago he went away to purchase tea,
Leaving his lonely wife alone in empty boat;
Shrouded in moonlight, on the cold river I float.
Deep in the night I dreamed of happy bygone years
And woke to find my rouged face crisscrossed with tears."

Listening to her sad music, I sighed with pain;
Hearing her story, I sighed again and again.
"Both of us in misfortune go from shore to shore.
Meeting now, need we have known each other before?
I was banished from the capital last year
To live degraded and ill in this city here.
The city's too remote to know melodious song,
So I have never heard music the whole year long.
I dwell by riverbank on low and damp ground
In a house yellow reeds and stunted bamboos surround.
What is here to be heard from daybreak till nightfall
But gibbons' cry and cuckoos' homeward-going call?
By blooming riverside and under autumn moon
I've often taken wine up and drunk it alone.
Of course I've mountain songs and village pipes to hear,
But they are crude and strident and grate on the ear.
Listening to you playing on pipa tonight,
With your music divine e'en my hearing seems bright.
Will you sit down and play for us a tune once more?
I'll write for you an ode to the pipa I adore."
Touched by what I said, the player stood for long,
Then sat down, tore at strings and played another song.
So sad, so drear, so different, it moved us deep;
All those who heard it hid the face and began to weep.
Of all the company at table who wept most?
It was none other than the exiled blue-robed host.

商人重利轻别离，前月浮梁买茶去。
去来江口守空船，绕船月明江水寒。
夜深忽梦少年事，梦啼妆泪红阑干。

我闻琵琶已叹息，又闻此语重唧唧。
同是天涯沦落人，相逢何必曾相识！
我从去年辞帝京，谪居卧病浔阳城。
浔阳地僻无音乐，终岁不闻丝竹声。
住近湓江地低湿，黄芦苦竹绕宅生。
其间旦暮闻何物？杜鹃啼血猿哀鸣。
春江花朝秋月夜，往往取酒还独倾。
岂无山歌与村笛？呕哑嘲哳难为听。
今夜闻君琵琶语，如听仙乐耳暂明。
莫辞更坐弹一曲，为君翻作琵琶行。
感我此言良久立，却坐促弦弦转急。
凄凄不似向前声，满座重闻皆掩泣。
座中泣下谁最多？江州司马青衫湿。

A Flower in the Haze

In bloom, she's not a flower;
Hazy, she's not a haze.
She comes at midnight hour;
She goes with starry rays.
She comes like vernal dreams that cannot stay
And goes like morning clouds that melt away.

The Last Look at the Peonies at Night

I'm saddened by the courtyard peonies brilliant red;
At dusk but two of them are left and withered.
I am afraid they can't survive the morning blast;*
By lantern light I take a look, the long, long last.

---

* Weng Xianliang's translation versified.

花非花

花非花，雾非雾，夜半来，天明去。
来如春梦几多时？去似朝云无觅处。

惜牡丹花

惆怅阶前红牡丹，晚来唯有两枝残。
明朝风起应吹尽，夜惜衰红把火看。

The Pavilion of Swallows (I)*

After Zhang Zhongsu's poems, using the same rhyme scheme.

Her room is drowned in moonlight and the screen in frost;
The quilt grows cold with dying lamp; she makes her bed.
The moonlit night in which Swallows' Pavilion's lost
Lengthens since autumn came for one who mourns the dead.

The Pavilion of Swallows (II)

Her silken dress with golden flowers fades like smoke;
She tries to put it on, but soon she melts in tears.
Since she's no longer danced to the air of "Rainbow Cloak,"
It's been stored in the chest for ten long years.

* See Zhang Zhongsu's "Pavilion of Swallows."

燕子楼（其一）

满窗明月满帘霜，被冷灯残拂卧床。
燕子楼中霜月夜，秋来只为一人长。

燕子楼（其二）

钿晕罗衫色似烟，几回欲著即潸然。
自从不舞霓裳曲，叠在空箱十一年。

The Pavilion of Swallows (III)

Some friends come back from ancient capital and say
They've visited the grave of her dear lord again.
The graveyard poplar white grows high as pillar grey.
How can her rosy face still beautiful remain!

Sunset and Moonrise on the River

The last departing rays pave their way on the river;
Half its waves turn red and all the others shiver.
How I pity the third night of the ninth month, alas!
The moon looks like a bow, dewdrops like pearls on grass.

燕子楼（其三）

今春有客洛阳回，曾到尚书墓上来。
见说白杨堪作柱，争教红粉不成灰。

暮江吟

一道残阳铺水中，半江瑟瑟半江红。
可怜九月初三夜，露似真珠月似弓。

LI SHEN
(780-846)

The Peasants (I)

Each seed that's sown in spring,
Will make autumn yields high.
What will fertile fields bring?
Of hunger peasants die.

The Peasants (II)

At noon they hoe up weeds;
Their sweat drips on the soil.
Who knows the rice that feeds
Is the fruit of hard toil!

李绅
（780–846）

悯农二首（其一）

春种一粒粟，秋收万颗子。
四海无闲田，农夫犹饿死。

悯农二首（其二）

锄禾日当午，汗滴禾下土。
谁知盘中餐，粒粒皆辛苦。

LIU ZONGYUAN
(773-819)

Fishing in Snow

From hill to hill no bird in flight,
From path to path no man in sight.
A straw-cloak'd man afloat, behold!
Is fishing snow on river cold.

柳宗元
（773–819）

江雪

千山鸟飞绝，
万径人踪灭。
孤舟蓑笠翁，
独钓寒江雪。

Drinking*

I fill my cup with drink divine;
It is another boring day.
First let me drink to Lord of Wine,
Who helps to drive the blues away.

One draught and different I feel;
At once the world revives anew;
The hidden hills themselves reveal;
The river takes on warming hue.

Exuberant the southern gate;
Trees raise their leafy arms so nice;
With shade their roots are saturate;
All night you hear silent advice.

So drink your fill and do not stop!
Drunk, you may lie on fragrant grass.
Rich revelers in the wine shop,
What have you in your cups, alas!

* Weng Xianliang's translation versified.

饮酒

今夕少愉乐，起坐开清樽。
举觞酹先酒，为我驱忧烦。
须臾心自殊，顿觉天地暄。
连山变幽晦，绿水函晏温。
蔼蔼南郭门，树木一何繁。
清阴可自庇，竟夕闻佳言。
尽醉无复辞，偃卧有芳荪。
彼哉晋楚富，此道未必存。

LI SHE
(Dates Unknown)

Lodging Again at the Southern Pass

I've left the capital to go far, far away,
And pass the Southern Town with mountains high and low.
The cold stream's water, which the city gate can't stay,
Flows all night long, murmuring about my woe.

李涉

（生卒年不详）

再宿武关

远别秦城万里游，

乱山高下出商州。

关门不锁寒溪水，

一夜潺湲送客愁。

CUI JIAO
(Dates Unknown)

To the Maid of My Aunt*

The sons of prince and lord all try to find thy trace;
Thy scarf is wet with tears streaming down thy face.
The mansion where thou enter is deep as the sea;
Thy master from now on is a stranger to thee.

* The poet loved his aunt's maid, who was later married to a rich lord. On reading this poem, the lord sent her back to the poet.

崔郊
（生卒年不详）

赠婢

公子王孙逐后尘，
绿珠垂泪滴罗巾。
侯门一入深如海，
从此萧郎是路人。

YUAN ZHEN
(779-831)

To My Deceased Wife (II)

One day we said for fun, "What if one of us dies?"
But now it has all come to pass before my eyes.
Your clothes nearly all have been given away;
I cannot bear to see your needlework today.
Remembering your kindness, I'm kind to your maids;
Dreaming of you, to your friends I give friendly aids.
I know death is a sorrow no one can ignore,
But a poor couple like us have more to deplore.

At an Old Palace

Deserted now imperial bowers.
For whom still redden palace flowers?
Some white-haired chambermaids at leisure
Talk of the late emperor's* pleasure.

* Emperor Xuan Zong (reigned 725-768) of the Tang Dynasty, who loved the beautiful Lady Yang Yuhuan (719-756). See Bai Ju-yi's long poem "The Everlasting Regret."

元稹

（779–831）

遣悲怀三首（其二）

昔日戏言身后意，今朝都到眼前来。
衣裳已施行看尽，针线犹存未忍开。
尚想旧情怜婢仆，也曾因梦送钱财。
诚知此恨人人有，贫贱夫妻百事哀。

行宫

寥落古行宫，宫花寂寞红。
白头宫女在，闲坐说玄宗。

Chrysanthemum

Around the cottage like Tao's* autumn flowers grow;
Along the hedge I stroll until the sun hangs low.
Not that I favor partially the chrysanthemum,
But it's the flower; after it none will come.

Thinking of My Dear Departed**

No water's wide enough when you have crossed the sea;
No cloud is beautiful but that which crowns the peak.
I pass by flowers that fail to attract poor me
Half for your sake and half for Taoism I seek.

* Tao Qian (c. 365-427) who loved the chrysanthemum.

** The poet was heart-broken after his wife's death and would retire from the world in accordance with the teaching of Taoism, so he was no longer attracted by beautiful flowers.

菊花

秋丛绕舍似陶家，遍绕篱边日渐斜。
不是花中偏爱菊，此花开尽更无花。

离思

曾经沧海难为水，除却巫山不是云。
取次花丛懒回顾，半缘修道半缘君。

JIA DAO
(779-843)

My Lord's Garden*

A thousand homes are shattered; a garden's laid out;
Roses grow everywhere, but no fruit-bearing trees.
When blows the autumn wind and roses fall about,
In the thorn-choked pavilion can you sit at ease?

A Note Left for an Absent Recluse

I ask your lad beneath a tree.
"My master's gone for herbs," says he,
"Amid the hills I know not where,
For clouds have veiled them here and there."

* Weng Xianliang's translation versified.

贾岛
（779–843）

题兴化寺园亭

破却千家作一池，不栽桃李种蔷薇。
蔷薇花落秋风起，荆棘满亭君自知。

访隐者不遇

松下问童子，言师采药去。
只在此山中，云深不知处。

ZHANG HU
(?-849)

Swan Song

Homesick a thousand miles away,
Shut in deep palace twenty years.
Singing the dying swan's sweet lay,
Oh, how can she hold back her tears!

张祜

（ ？ –849 ）

何满子

故国三千里，

深宫二十年。

一声何满子，

双泪落君前。

LIU ZAO
(Dates Unknown)

Farther North*

Ten long, long winters in northern town I did stay;
My heart cried out for home in the south night and day.
Now as I cross the river, farther north I roam;
My heart cries out for northern town as for my home.

* Weng Xianliang's translation versified.

刘皂
（生卒年不详）

旅次朔方

客舍并州已十霜，
归心日夜忆咸阳。
无端更渡桑干水，
却望并州是故乡。

HUANGFU SONG
(Dates Unknown)

Tune: "Dreaming of the South"

Out candles burned;
Dark on the screen red cannas turned.
I dreamed of mume fruit ripening on southern shore,
Of flute songs played in boat one rainy night of yore,
Of whispered farewell lost
In running stream below the bridge beside the post.

皇甫松
（生卒年不详）

梦江南

兰烬落，屏上暗红蕉。
闲梦江南梅熟日，夜船吹笛雨萧萧。
人语驿边桥。

ZHU QINGYU
(Dates Unknown)

To an Examiner on the Eve of Examination*

Last night red candles burned bright in the bridal room;
At dawn she'll kowtow to new parents with the groom.
She whispers to him after touching up her face:
"Have I painted my brows with fashionable grace?"

* The poet asks the examiner whether his work is up to the standard of the civil service examination.

朱庆馀
（生卒年不详）

近试上张水部

洞房昨夜停红烛，
待晓堂前拜舅姑。
妆罢低声问夫婿：
画眉深浅入时无？

LI HE
(790-816)

Twenty-three Horse Poems (I)

A string of coins upon his back, noble and proud,
His hoofs silvery white as though born to trot in cloud.
But where's the whip of gold, the saddle cloth of brocade?
The cloth is not yet woven; the whip not yet made.

Twenty-three Horse Poems (IV)

This is no ordinary steed
But an incarnate star indeed.
When I tap his bony frame, what's found?
I seem to hear metallic sound.

李贺
（790–816）

马诗二十三首（其一）

龙脊贴连钱，银蹄白踏烟。
无人织锦韂，谁为铸金鞭。

马诗二十三首（其四）

此马非凡马，房星本是星。
向前敲瘦骨，犹自带铜声。

Twenty-three Horse Poems (V)

The desert sands look white as snow;
The crescent moon hangs like a bow.
When would the steed in golden gear
Gallop all night through autumn clear?

Twenty-three Horse Poems (XXIII)

"I'll have elixir," Emperor Wu says,
And heaps of gold go up in purple haze.
All steeds in royal stable, ah, must die,
For none of them can run up to the sky.

马诗二十三首（其五）

大漠沙如雪，燕山月似钩。

何当金络脑，快走踏清秋。

马诗二十三首
（其二十三）

武帝爱神仙，烧金得紫烟。

厩中皆肉马，不解上青天。

XU NING
(Dates Unknown)

To One in Yangzhou

Your bashful face could hardly bear the weight of tear;
Your long, long brows would easily feel sorrow near.
Of all the moonlit nights on earth when people part,
Two-thirds shed light upon Yangzhou with broken heart.

徐凝
（生卒年不详）

忆扬州

萧娘脸薄难胜泪，
桃叶眉长易觉愁。
天下三分明月夜，
二分无赖是扬州。

YONG YUZHI
(Dates Unknown)

To the Riverside Willow

Your long, long branches wave by riverside,
Your green, green leaves like wreaths of smoke afloat.
"Make ropes unbreakable of them," she sighed,
"To tie up my beloved one's parting boat!"

雍裕之
（生卒年不详）

江边柳

袅袅古堤边，
青青一树烟。
若为丝不断，
留取系郎船。

XU HUN
(Dates Unknown)

Gazing Afar in the Evening from the West Tower of Xianyang*

On city wall I see grief spread for miles and miles
O'er reeds and willow trees as planted on flats and isles.
The sun beneath the cloud sinks o'er waterside bower;
The wind before the storm fills the mountainside tower.
In the wasted Qin garden only birds fly still;
'Mid yellow leaves in Han** palace cicadas shrill.
O wayfarer, don't ask about the days gone by!
Coming from the east, I hear only the river sigh.

* Ancient capital of the Qin Dynasty (221-207 BC)
** The Han Dynasty (206 BC-AD 220).

许浑
（生卒年不详）

咸阳城西楼晚眺

一上高城万里愁，蒹葭杨柳似汀洲。
溪云初起日沉阁，山雨欲来风满楼。
鸟下绿芜秦苑夕，蝉鸣黄叶汉宫秋。
行人莫问当年事，故国东来渭水流。

DU MU
(803-852)

Ruined Splendor*

Rank grasses grow, Six Dynasties** splendor's no more.
The sky is lightly blue and clouds free as of yore.
Birds come and go into the gloom of wooded hills,
And songs and wails alike merge in murmuring rills.
Like countless window curtains falls late autumn rain,
High towers steeped in sunset, wind and flute's refrain.
Oh, how I miss the lakeside sage*** of bygone days!
I see but ancient trees loom ragged in the haze.

---

* Weng Xianliang's translation versified.
** The Six Southern Dynasties (221-280; 317-589).
*** Fan Li, who retired at the zenith of his political career after the Kingdom of Yue conquered the Kingdom of Wu in 473 BC

杜牧

（803–852）

题宣州开元寺水阁，阁下宛溪，夹溪居人

六朝文物草连空，天淡云闲今古同。

鸟去鸟来山色里，人歌人哭水声中。

深秋帘幕千家雨，落日楼台一笛风。

惆怅无日见范蠡，参差烟树五湖东。

Spring Abides Not

Spring days half gone to the year's end amount,
For all the other seasons do not count.
I drink to flowers loath to say adieu
And feel e'en wine would taste like winter brew.
I am distressed after the parting cup
The broom will sweep all fallen petals up.
From year to year thus life will pass away
Alas! There's no one who its course can stay!

惜春

春半年已除，其余强为有。

即此醉残花，便同尝腊酒。

怅望送春杯，殷勤扫花帚。

谁为驻东流，年年长在手。

Moored on River Qinhuai*

Cold water veiled in mist and shores in dim moonlight,
I moor on River Qinhuai near wine shops at night,
Where songstress knowing not the grief of conquered land,
Still sings the songs composed by a captive ruler's hand. **

Parting

Deep, deep our love, too deep to show.
Deep, deep we drink; silent we grow.
The candle grieves to see us part;
It melts in tears with burnt-out heart.

The Day of Mourning for the Dead***

The day of mourning for the dead it's raining hard;
My heart is broken on my way to the graveyard.
Where can I find a wine shop to drown my sad hours?
A herdboy points to cots amid apricot flowers.

---

* In present-day Nanjing, ancient capital of the Chen Dynasty (557-589).
** The last ruler of Chen was taken captive in 589.
*** The fourth or fifth day of April, when Chinese people used to visit their ancestral burial mounds.

泊秦淮

烟笼寒水月笼沙，夜泊秦淮近酒家。

商女不知亡国恨，隔江犹唱后庭花。

赠别

多情却似总无情，唯觉樽前笑不成。

蜡烛有心还惜别，替人垂泪到天明。

清明

清明时节雨纷纷，路上行人欲断魂。

借问酒家何处有？牧童遥指杏花村。

YONG TAO
(805-?)

The Bridge of Love's End

Why should this bridge be called Love's End,
Since love without an end will last?
Plant willow trees for parting friend;
Your longing for him will stand fast.*

* The last two lines were rewritten by the versifier.

雍陶

（805–？）

题情尽桥

从来只有情难尽，
何事名为情尽桥。
自此改名为折柳，
任他离恨一条条。

LI CHEN ET AL.*

To a Waterfall

You are not tired while passing o'er a thousand crags;
I can see from afar your source in sky-high caves.
You cannot be retained by brooks or creeks or jags;
At last you will return among the ocean waves.

* The first two lines were written by a monk and the last two by Li Chen, Emperor Xuan Zong of the Tang Dynasty.

李忱 等

瀑布联句

千岩万壑不辞劳，

远看方知出处高。

溪涧岂能留得住，

终归大海作波涛。

WEN TINGYUN
(813-870)

Tune: "Buddhist Dancers"

See light and shade upon her eyebrows' double peaks
And cloud-tike hair overshadow her snow-white cheeks.
Idly she rises to pencil her brows;
Slowly she makes up, feeling still the drowse.

In mirrors back and front she's eying,
Her face with blooms in beauty vying.
On broidered silken vest she wears
There're golden partridges in pairs.

温庭筠

（813–870）

菩萨蛮

小山重叠金明灭，鬓云欲度香腮雪。

懒起画蛾眉，弄妆梳洗迟。

照花前后镜，花面交相映。

新帖绣罗襦，双双金鹧鸪。

Tune: "Song of Water Clock at Night"

The tearful candle red
And fragrant censer spread
Within the painted bower a gloomy autumn tight.
Worn eyebrows penciled
And hair disheveled,
She feels her quilt the colder and longer the night.

The lonely withered trees
And midnight rain and breeze
Don't care about her bitter parting sorrow.
Leaf on leaf without grief,
Drop by drop without stop,
They fall on vacant steps until the morrow.

Tune: "Dreaming of the South"

After dressing my hair,
Alone I climb the stair.
On the railings I lean
To view the river scene.
A thousand sails pass by,
But not the one for which wait I.
The slanting sun sheds sympathetic ray;
The carefree river carries it away.
My heart breaks at the sight
Of the islet with duckweed white.*

* Place where people used to bid farewell.

更漏子·玉炉香

玉炉香，红蜡泪，偏照画堂秋思。
眉翠薄，鬓云残，夜长衾枕寒。

梧桐树，三更雨，不道离情正苦。
一叶叶，一声声，空阶滴到明。

望江南

梳洗罢，独倚望江楼。
过尽千帆皆不是，斜晖脉脉水悠悠。
肠断白蘋洲。

CHEN TAO
(812-885)

The Riverside Battleground

They would lay down their lives to wipe away the Huns;
They've bit the dust, five thousand sable-clad brave ones.
Alas! Their bones lie on riverside battleground,
But in dreams of their wives they still seem safe and sound.

陈陶

（812–885）

陇西行

誓扫匈奴不顾身，
五千貂锦丧胡尘。
可怜无定河边骨，
犹是春闺梦里人。

LI SHANGYIN
(812-858)

The Sad Zither

Why should the zither sad have fifty strings?
Each string, each strain evokes but vanished springs:
Dim morning dream to be a butterfly;
Amorous heart poured out in cuckoo's cry.
In moonlit pearls see tears in mermaid's eyes;
From sunburnt emerald let vapor rise.
Such feeling cannot be recalled again;
It seemed long lost e'en when it was felt then.

On the Plain of Tombs*

At dusk my heart is filled with gloom;
I drive my cab to ancient tomb.
The setting sun appears sublime,
But O! 'Tis near its dying time.

* The Merrymaking Plain was situated to the south of the capital (present-day Xi'an), where the tombs of five emperors of the Han Dynasty (206 BC-AD 220) were.

李商隐
（812–858）

锦瑟

锦瑟无端五十弦，一弦一柱思华年。
庄生晓梦迷蝴蝶，望帝春心托杜鹃。
沧海月明珠有泪，蓝田日暖玉生烟。
此情可待成追忆，只是当时已惘然。

乐游原

向晚意不适，驱车登古原。
夕阳无限好，只是近黄昏。

To One Unnamed (I)

You said you'd come, but you are gone and left no trace;
I wake to hear in moonlit tower the fifth watch bell.
In dream my cry couldn't call you back from distant place;
In haste with ink unthickened I cannot write well.
The candlelight illumines half our broidered bed;
The smell of musk still faintly sweetens lotus screen.
Beyond my reach the far-off fairy mountains spread,
But you're still farther off than fairy mountains green.

无题（其一）

来是空言去绝踪，月斜楼上五更钟。
梦为远别啼难唤，书被催成墨未浓。
蜡照半笼金翡翠，麝熏微度绣芙蓉。
刘郎已恨蓬山远，更隔蓬山一万重！

To One Unnamed (II)

The rustling eastern wind came with a drizzle light,
And thunder faintly rolled beyond the lotus pool.
When doors were locked and incense burned, I came at night
And went at dawn when windlass pulled up water cool.*
You peeped at me first from behind a curtained bower;
I'm left at last with but the cushion of a dame.
Let my desire not bloom and vie with vernal flower!
For inch by inch my heart is consumed by the flame.

* The poet had a tryst with an unnamed lover.

无题（其二）

飒飒东风细雨来，芙蓉塘外有轻雷。

金蟾啮锁烧香入，玉虎牵丝汲井回。

贾氏窥帘韩掾少，宓妃留枕魏王才。

春心莫共花争发，一寸相思一寸灰！

To One Unnamed (III)

It's difficult for us to meet and hard to part;
The east wind is too weak to revive flowers dead.
Spring silkworm till its death spins silk from lovesick heart,
And candles but when burned up have no tears to shed.
At dawn I'm grieved to think your mirrored hair turns grey;
At night you would feel cold while I croon by moonlight.
To the three fairy hills it is not a long way.
Would the blue birds oft fly to see you on the height!

无题（其三）

相见时难别亦难，东风无力百花残。
春蚕到死丝方尽，蜡炬成灰泪始干。
晓镜但愁云鬓改，夜吟应觉月光寒。
蓬山此去无多路，青鸟殷勤为探看。

LI QUNYU
(813-860)

To a Deserted Lover

Your literary fame was once loved best;
Your muse then came in dreams to lovebirds' nest.
We cannot rule o'er fickle cloud or shower,
So let it water any thirsting flower!*

* Rewritten by the versifier.

李群玉

（813–860）

赠人

曾留宋玉旧衣裳，

惹得巫山梦里香。

云雨无情难管领，

任他别嫁楚襄王。

CUI JUE
(Dates Unknown)

Elegy on Li Shangyin

In vain you could have soared to the azure sky;
Before you could fulfill your ambition you die.
The birds bewail with fallen flower: "Where are you?"
The phoenix won't alight on dead tree or bamboo.
A horse'd be crippled if not trained by riders good;
The lutist broke his lute for one who understood.
In nether world not sun or moon or stars in sight,
But you're the brightest star in the eternal night.

崔珏
（生卒年不详）

哭李商隐

虚负凌云万丈才，一生襟抱未曾开。
鸟啼花落人何在，竹死桐枯凤不来。
良马足因无主踠，旧交心为绝弦哀。
九泉莫叹三光隔，又送文星入夜台。

ZHAO JIA
(Dates Unknown)

On the Riverside Tower

Alone I mount the Riverside Tower and sigh
To see the moonbeams blend with waves and waves with sky.
Last year I came to view the moon with my compeers.
But where are they, now that the scene is like last year's?

赵嘏
（生卒年不详）

江楼感旧

独上江楼思渺然，
月光如水水如天。
同来望月人何处？
风景依稀似去年。

CAO YE
(816-875)

The Rats in the Public Granary

The rats in the public granary so fatted grow,
When they see man come in, they do not run away.
The soldiers not provided, the people hungry go.
Who allows them to eat so much from day to day?

曹邺
（816–875）

官仓鼠

官仓老鼠大如斗，
见人开仓亦不走。
健儿无粮百姓饥，
谁遣朝朝入君口？

LUO YIN
(833-909)

To a Singing Girl

Drunken, we parted here more than ten years ago.
Now again I meet you as beautiful as then.
You are not married and my fame remains low;
Maybe we are not equal to all other men.

For Myself

Sing when you're happy and from worries keep away!
How can we bear so much regret and so much sorrow?
When you have wine to drink, oh, drink your fill today!
Should sorrow come, alas! Tell it to come tomorrow!

罗隐

（833–909）

赠妓云英

钟陵醉别十余春，重见云英掌上身。
我未成名卿未嫁，可能俱是不如人。

自遣

得即高歌失即休，多愁多恨亦悠悠。
今朝有酒今朝醉，明日愁来明日愁。

To the Parrot

Do not complain of golden cage and wings cut short;
The southern land is far warmer than the northwest.*
Don't clearly speak, if you listen to my exhort!
You can't be free if clearly your complaint's expressed.

Snow

All say that snow forebodes a bumper year.
What if it should arouse less joy than fear?
There are poor people in the capital
Who are afraid a bumper snow will fall.

* The poet went from the northwest to the south just as the parrot did.

鹦鹉

莫恨雕笼翠羽残，江南地暖陇西寒。
劝君不用分明语，语得分明出转难。

雪

尽道丰年瑞，丰年事若何？
长安有贫者，为瑞不宜多。

WEI ZHUANG
(836-910)

Tune: "Song of a Lady's Crown" (I)

The seventeenth of fourth month comes anew.
It was this day last year
I parted from you.
Holding back tear after tear,
Bashfully you pretended to bow
And drew together half your brow.

Not knowing that my heart is broken,
I follow you in dreams awoken.
None knows how sad am I
But the moon in the sky.

韦庄

（836–910）

女冠子（其一）

四月十七，正是去年今日。
别君时，忍泪佯低面，含羞半敛眉。

不知魂已断，空有梦相随。
除却天边月，没人知。

Tune: "Song of a Lady's Crown" (II)

Last night at middle hour
I dreamed of you who whispered on my pillow,
Your face still fair as peach-tree flower,
Your downcast brows like leaves of willow.

Half shy, half glad,
You'd go away but stop to stay.
I woke to find the dream so sad,
A grief not to allay.

女冠子（其二）

昨夜夜半，枕上分明梦见。
语多时，依旧桃花面，频低柳叶眉。

半羞还半喜，欲去又依依。
觉来知是梦，不胜悲。

HUANG CHAO
(?-884)*

To the Chrysanthemum

In soughing western wind you blossom far and nigh;
Your fragrance is too cold to invite butterfly.
Some day if I as Lord of Spring come into power,
I'll order you to bloom together with peach flower.

The Chrysanthemum

When autumn comes, Mountain-Climbing Day** is nigh;
My flower blows when others' season terminates.
All o'er the capital my fragrance rises sky high;
You'll see the city clad in golden amour plates.

* Huang Chao was the leader of the peasant uprising at the end of the Tang Dynasty (618-907).
** The ninth day of the ninth lunar month.

黄巢
（？ –884）

题菊花

飒飒西风满院栽，蕊寒香冷蝶难来。
他年我若为青帝，报与桃花一处开。

菊花

待到秋来九月八，我花开后百花杀。
冲天香阵透长安，满城尽带黄金甲。

NIE YIZHONG
(837-884)

Poor Peasants

Up in old fields the fathers toil;
Down in new fields the sons break soil.
The corn in sixth moon still in blade,
Government granaries are made.

聂夷中

（*837–884*）

田家

父耕原上田，

子劚山下荒。

六月禾未秀，

官家已修仓。

ZHANG JIE
(837- ?)

The Pit Where Emperor Qin* Burned the Classics

Smoke of burnt classics gone up with the empire's fall,
Fortress and rivers could not guard the capital.
Before the pit turned cold, eastern rebellion spread;
The leaders of revolt were not scholars well read.

* The First Emperor of the Qin Dynasty ordered all classics burned and 460 scholars buried alive in 213 BC

章碣
（837–?）

焚书坑

竹帛烟销帝业虚，
关河空锁祖龙居。
坑灰未冷山东乱，
刘项原来不读书。

CAO SONG
(828-903)

A Year of War

The lakeside country has become a battleground.
How can the peasants and woodmen live all around?
I pray you not to talk about the glories vain;
A victor's fame is built on bones of soldiers slain.

曹松
（828–903）

己亥岁

泽国江山入战图，
生民何计乐樵苏？
凭君莫话封侯事，
一将功成万骨枯。

CUI DAORONG
(880-907)

A Cloak of Spring

I try to cut for him a cloak of spring;
My scissors breathe the cold still lingering.
Far colder is the far-off garrison town.
How can he not expect a warrior's gown!

崔道融
（*880–907*）

春闺

欲剪宜春字，
春寒入剪刀。
辽阳在何处，
莫望寄征袍。

JIN CHANGXU
(Dates Unknown)

A Complaint in Spring

Drive orioles off the tree;
Their songs awake poor me
From dreaming of my dear
Far off on the frontier.

金昌绪
（生卒年不详）

春怨

打起黄莺儿，
莫教枝上啼。
啼时惊妾梦，
不得到辽西。

WANG JIA
(851-?)

After the Rain

Before the rain I still see blooming flowers;
Only green leaves are left after the showers.
Over the wall pass butterflies and bees;
I wonder whether spring's in next-door trees.

王驾
（851–?）

雨晴

雨前初见花间蕊，
雨后全无叶底花。
蜂蝶纷纷过墙去，
却疑春色在邻家。

ZHANG BI
(Dates Unknown)

To My Love

When you were gone, in my dream I lingered you know where.
The courtyard seemed the same with zigzag rails around.
Only the sympathetic moon was shining there
For me alone on flowers fallen on the ground.

张泌
（生卒年不详）

寄人

别梦依依到谢家，
小廊回合曲阑斜。
多情只有春庭月，
犹为离人照落花。

ANONYMOUS

The Golden Dress

Love not your golden dress, I pray,
More than your youthful golden hours.
Gather sweet blossoms while you may
And not the twig devoid of flowers!

无名氏

金缕衣

劝君莫惜金缕衣，
劝君惜取少年时。
花开堪折直须折，
莫待无花空折枝。

图书在版编目（CIP）数据

不朽的美：云想衣裳花想容：许渊冲经典英译诗词：唐朝．第二辑：汉英对照 / 许渊冲译．-- 北京：新世界出版社，2019.6（2021.6 重印）
ISBN 978-7-5104-6280-1

Ⅰ．①不… Ⅱ．①许… Ⅲ．①古典诗歌—诗集—中国—汉、英 Ⅳ．① I222

中国版本图书馆 CIP 数据核字 (2017) 第 100903 号

Songs of the Immortals

AN ANTHOLOGY OF CLASSICAL CHINESE POETRY (II)

不朽的美：云想衣裳花想容

许渊冲经典英译诗词（唐朝）

第二辑：汉英对照

译　　者：许渊冲
审　　定：王池英
责任编辑：李晨曦
特邀编辑：杨晓敏
装帧设计：贺玉婷
责任校对：宣　慧　陆诗婷
责任印制：王宝根　苏爱玲
出　　版：新世界出版社
网　　址：http://www.nwp.com.cn
社　　址：北京西城区百万庄大街 24 号（100037）
发 行 部：(010)6899 5968（电话）　(010)6899 0635（电话）
总 编 室：(010)6899 5424（电话）　(010)6832 6679（传真）
版 权 部：+8610 6899 6306（电话）nwpcd@sina.com（电邮）
印　　刷：北京亚通印刷有限责任公司
经　　销：新华书店
开　　本：880mm × 1230mm　1/32　尺寸：145mm × 210mm
字　　数：150 千字　　印张：10.125
版　　次：2019 年 6 月第 1 版　2021 年 6 月第 2 次印刷
书　　号：ISBN 978-7-5104-6280-1
定　　价：48.00 元